WOMEN'S SILENCE
MEN'S VIOLENCE

ANNA CLARK

■ **Anna Clark** is an active member of the London Feminist History Group. She was graduated from Radcliffe College, Harvard University and received her M.A. from the University of Essex. She is currently a fellow of the Social Science Research Council, New York, while she writes a dissertation for Rutgers University, New Jersey, on popular morality and the construction of gender in London. Anna Clark has written an article in *The Progress of Romance*, edited by Jean Radford (RKP, 1986) and another article in *The Sexual Dynamics of History*, edited by the London Feminist History Group (Pluto, 1983).

D0920267

William Ashton rescuing Mary Wood
from the Squire. © The British Library

WOMEN'S SILENCE
MEN'S VIOLENCE

SEXUAL ASSAULT IN ENGLAND 1770-1845

ANNA CLARK

PANDORA

London and New York

First published in 1987 by Pandora Press
(Routledge & Kegan Paul Ltd)
11 New Fetter Lane, London EC4P 4EE

Published in the USA by
Pandora Press
(Routledge & Kegan Paul Inc.)
in association with Methuen Inc.
29 West 35th Street, New York, NY 10001

Set in Plantin, 10 on 11½ pt
by Columns of Reading
and printed in the British Isles
by The Guernsey Press Co Ltd
Guernsey, Channel Islands

Library of Congress Cataloging in Publication Data

Clark, Anna.
Women's silence, men's violence.
Bibliography: p.
Includes index.
1. Rape – England – History – 18th century.   2. Rape –
England – History – 19th century.   3. England – Moral con-
ditions.
HV6569.G72E534   1986   364.1'532'0942   86-9299

British Library CIP Data also available

ISBN 0-86358-103-X

Contents

Acknowledgments

I am very grateful to the many people who have been kind enough to listen to or read various versions of this work as it has evolved through many changes over five years. First, my appreciation to Leonore Davidoff for the inspiration of her own work and her dedicated supervision of my MA thesis, from which this book germinated. Raphael Samuel, Jan Lambertz, Barbara Taylor, Alison Oram, and Barbara Brookes also read chapters and discussed ideas with me during that time. I would also like to thank the Knox Fellowship, Radcliffe College, Rutgers University, and my grandmother, Mrs. F.M. Smith, for financial support of my research. At Rutgers University, John Gillis, Suzanne Lebsock, Polly Beals, Carolyn Strange, Adrienne Scerback, and Laura Tabili have provided many useful comments and warm support. Judith Walkowitz has read several versions of this work, clarifying it with her astute comments. The London Feminist History Group has twice heard papers on various stages of my research; its members' responses and criticisms were always crucial. The Rutgers History Department Women's History Seminar has also been a continually perceptive audience for my work, and the New York University Graduate Women's Studies Group's vigorous critique of my second chapter enlivened its revision. Margaret Hunt provided invaluable help for eighteenth-century London and Sian Moore gave me many useful references for Yorkshire life. My father, Dr David Clark, and my mother, Sylvia Smith Clark, have always been helpful and encouraging. Deborah Mabbett clarified my ideas for the final revision and Dena Leiter has helped me live in twentieth-century New Jersey as well as nineteenth-century London. Finally, responsibility for the flaws in my analysis, of course, remains my own.

CHAPTER 1

Introduction: feminist theory in historical perspective

All women know the paralyzing fear of walking down a dark street at night, hearing mysterious footsteps clicking behind, wondering whether the night out was worth these moments of terror . . the dread that strikes us when we hear that a woman has been raped in our neighbourhood . . . the sudden resolve to be more cautious, not to accept the offers of dubious men to walk us home, or not to go out at night at all.

It seems to be a fact of life that the fear of rape imposes a curfew on our movements; a fact that if we stay at home we will be safe, but if we venture out alone we face the strange rapist in the dark alley.

These fears and restrictions, however, do not derive from common-sense caution. By limiting our own freedom, we obey the dictates of a myth – a myth which covertly warns us that rapists punish women who stray from the proper place. This book identifies the myth of rape as a historical invention.

As Susan Brownmiller has shown, by identifying strangers and deviants as rapists this myth enables other men to extort submission from women in exchange for protection; it is the biggest protection racket the world has ever known. Of course, the protection the myth offers in exchange for obedience is illusory. Study after study has shown that today women face as much, if not more danger in their own homes than on dark streets, and that rapists are male acquaintances or friends as often as threatening strangers.[1] This private terror intensifies the public fear of rape.

Did women enjoy freedom from this fear in the past?

1

Unfortunately, the answer is no. This book will show that in eighteenth-century England, both country and city women faced the danger of rape everywhere, and from every kind of man. Yet the protection racket of rape only became prevalent in the early nineteenth century, when sexual danger increasingly became the excuse to restrict women's freedom.

This book takes the basic feminist theory on rape, as developed by Brownmiller and others, and applies it to the period 1770–1845, an era of dramatic change which witnessed the Industrial Revolution and the rise of Victorianism. By understanding rape in historical perspective, we can better understand the problem of sexual violence in our own times. The nineteenth-century protection racket actually stemmed from middle-class efforts to control the activities of working women in public space. This fact illuminates today's debates on police control of the streets, revealing that it is not only an issue of race and class, but gender too. The use of rape as warning was also linked with an increasing stress on sexual purity as the measure of a woman's worth. A pure woman could not speak on sexual matters; therefore, she could not protest against rape. This shows how important it has been for feminists to assert the link between our freedom from sexual violence on the one hand, and on the other, our freedom to speak out on sex and to seek sexual pleasure.

In this introduction, I will demonstrate how feminist theory on rape illuminates women's experience of sexual violence in the past, while at the same time, the historical perspective sheds new light on contemporary feminist analysis.

Brownmiller's pathbreaking book *Against Our Will* contains many historical chapters, but her recounting of atrocities committed on women throughout the ages only serves to illustrate her fundamental point that 'since prehistoric times' men's power to use their 'biological tool' kept 'all women in a constant state of intimidation'.[2] However, rape is not an unchanging consequence of male biology, for the way sexual violence functions as a means of patriarchal domination, and indeed patriarchy itself, varies historically. Sometimes economic deprivation, or political powerlessness, may be more important features in the repression of women; at other points violence, and sexual violence, come to the foreground as a means of male domination.[3] The myth of rape as warning to women to behave is widely disseminated at times of great social change: today, it is part of a backlash aimed to push women into the home; in the early nineteenth century, it stemmed from the new notion of the home as a feminine private sphere.

In the late eighteenth century, the streets of London and country highways were seen as dangerous for everyone, and the danger of rape was not new. Then as now, women were raped as often by men they knew as by strangers, at home and at work as well as outdoors. Yet I have found no evidence in eighteenth-century pamphlets, court records, or newspapers that incidents of rape were used to warn women to stay out of public space. Rape was just one of the many ways in which women were oppressed. Heavy labour for poor wages, political powerlessness, and widespread non-sexual male violence kept women subordinate as well. The plight of working women excited little concern.

By the turn of the century, however, sexual danger became the focus of intensified attention on the place of women in public space. Magistrates, judges, and journalists dealing with rape cases began to introduce the idea that rape emperilled women's safety in evening streets; while men could travel freely, 'respectable' women would be safe only at home. Reformers portrayed factory work as fraught with the perils of seduction and violation. These notions helped enforce the burgeoning bourgeois ideology of separate spheres: that women belonged in the domestic sphere of the home, nurturant but sheltered, while men braved the hurly-burly of the marketplace and the streets.

The restrictive moral standards of separate spheres contrasted with the greater sexual and economic independence of working women. Middle-class reformers wished to see women at home and the poor at work; they abhorred the thought of either party enjoying the freedom of the streets. The attempts to intimidate women away from public space thus stemmed from the same roots as the repression of working-class street culture. Middle-class reformers, moreover, saw sexual danger as inherent in working women themselves. They confused seduction – surrender to one's passions – with rape – an uninvited assault, and regarded the victim of sexual danger as tainted herself.

These men believed that women who were raped had somehow invited assault by their insubordinate behaviour. This myth intensified the effect of individual male violence a thousand-fold by terrorizing all women; it helped to enforce women's status as chaste by encouraging them to stay at home under the putative protection of husband or father. The men who promulgated this myth were judges who questioned rape victims more severely than their assailants; doctors who claimed their expertise could determine the validity of a charge of sexual assault; poor law governors who sent unmarried mothers to workhouses; officials of charitable institutions who provided them with more religious propaganda than relief; and newspaper reporters who sensationally interpreted rapes as warnings to women to behave.

Through their expertise and institutional power these men enshrined their values into 'discourses'. 'Discourse' is most easily understood as merely a convenient, uniform term for various genres of speech or writing – the legal discourse, the medical discourse, and so on. The word has been popularized – but also mystified – by the French philosopher Foucault, who has been very influential in recent writings on sexuality. Foucault showed how power is exercised through discourses which define and therefore regulate and control the objects of their expertise – the criminal, the hospital patient, the madman, the homosexual. Before the modern era, he claimed, authorities physically punished deviant behaviour by such methods as branding, whipping, or even execution. In contrast, modern institutions attempted to punish and prevent criminal behaviour by studying the 'criminal personality', and reforming the mind rather than torturing the body. Foucault refuted the notion of Victorian sexual repression, arguing that the nineteenth century witnessed, not a silence about sex, but a proliferation of discourses about sexuality. These discourses defined the unmarried mother or the person who committed a homosexual act as a deviant: their sexuality totally encompassed their identity.[4] His ideas can be useful in assessing the treatment of the rape victim in the nineteenth century, as Susan Edwards has shown.[5] Doctors, lawyers, poor law officials and journalists all scrutinized the sexual behaviour of working women, and as a result, they regarded a woman who had been raped as a deviant rather than a victim.

Foucault, however, evaded and distorted central questions of power. He often wrote in the passive voice, obscuring who it was who exercised power, and in whose interests. As Leslie Stern aptly writes, 'one of the major functions of the myth of repression escapes him – the myth of repression has served to mask the oppression of women by men'.[6] Doctors and lawyers may have spawned endless writings about sex, but *women* were forbidden to speak about it in the early nineteenth century. These discourses reinforced and extended the effect of rape in expressing and perpetuating male domination.

Nonetheless, by focusing on the institutional basis of these discourses about rape, we can see how the British class situation affected the problem of sexual violence. American discourses about rape usually focus on the question of race: in fact, Angela Davis criticized Brownmiller's inadequate treatment of the Southern obsession with the black rapist, revealing that Southern whites only began lynching black men for alleged rape when black people gained political power after the American Civil War.[7] Myths about rape are thus engendered and manipulated by ruling elites at particular historical moments.

The reality of rape, however, transcends class boundaries; the use of rape as a warning to women ultimately benefits *all* men. While I have found almost no discussion of rape and race in Britain between 1770 and 1845, radicals popularized their own myth: the aristocratic libertine who sexually exploited poor working girls. But working women faced most danger of rape from men of their own class. The myth of the aristocratic libertine thus masked the reality of proletarian sexual violence. Poor men certainly suffered from class oppression under British justice, but when accused of rape they could take advantage of a judge's patriarchal bias by disparaging their victims as unchaste.

And the physical act of rape enables individual men of all classes to dominate women and violently to degrade and humiliate their victims. Because men use rape as a means of direct control over women, not primarily for sexual satisfaction, feminists such as Brownmiller have often declared that rape is a crime of violence, not sex.[8] For instance, in fifteenth-century Toulouse gangs of youths raped young women to force them into prostitution; in eighteenth-century France men raped their fiancées in a ritual of domination.[9]

Many feminists also stress that rape is an extension of the social construction of male sexuality as active, dominant and aggressive; in this sense, rape is sexual as well as violent.[10] Male sexuality, however, must be put into historical perspective in order to avoid the notion that men have always had a biological sex drive which compelled them to rape for sexual gratification.

In the late eighteenth century, a libertine discourse permeated slang and masculine popular culture, glorifying rape as a source of amusement, or a way of proving their masculinity to other men. While many eighteenth-century rakes prided themselves on seducing women with every technique but force, they often seemed to regard sex as the conquest of women, 'taking' her as if she were a precious jewel rather than a person desiring sexual pleasure herself. Such military metaphors blurred the distinction between rape and seduction. In the early nineteenth century, libertinism faded from public view, but continued as a private, subterranean stream; instead, men were told to be chivalrous and control their sexual desires. Yet chivalrous protection only extended to those women seen as chaste; and rape could be understood as a regrettable loss of self-control rather than a criminal act.

Of course, even as the social construction of masculine sexuality encouraged sexual aggression, rape was a capital crime up until 1841 and is still legally a very serious felony. The feminist analysis of female sexuality as property helps solve this paradox of simultaneous punishment and sanctioning of rape. Under patriarchy, narrowly defined here as the domination of husband or father over wife and children within the family, chastity defines a woman's value. Chastity ostensibly means a woman's virginity, or if married, fidelity; but this really comes down to her submission to the exclusive ownership of husband or father. As Lorenne Clark and Debra Lewis point out, if a woman seeks her own sexual pleasure, or if another man uses her sexually, she becomes damaged property, her exchangeable value threatened.[11]

These feminists have shown that the justice system only punishes rape if it infringes another man's property rights in a woman. But the notion of female sexuality as a thing, or as property, encourages men to believe they have a right to 'obtain' female sexuality: by paying for sex, as in prostitution or traditional marriage; by defrauding them as in seduction; or taking it by force, as in rape. If a woman did not behave in a chaste manner, she became fair game to any man. In the eighteenth century as in today, if a man believed he had a right to sex from a woman, and she refused, he could rape her, seeking sexual satisfaction and violent revenge despite her lack of consent. Men did not rape because they had an uncontrollable sexual urge; rather, men who raped believed that sex involved the 'taking' of women and that they had a right to women's sexuality. In a misogynist culture, as Brownmiller writes, 'a woman is perceived by the rapist both as a hated person and desired property.'[12]

Women are not 'property', of course; they are human beings with minds and wills of their own. Patriarchal ideology about rape attempted to force them to regard their sexuality as property, however, by using the threat of sexual violence to make women guard their chastity with their lives. Economically, if a woman could not earn a living for herself and her children, she needed to exchange her sexuality for subsistence, in marriage or in prostitution.

In late eighteenth-century England, however, the notion of women's sexuality as property was not universal. Some women could earn enough by their independent labour to live on their own and seek sexual pleasure rather than profit. As I will show in Chapter 2, this fact gave some women the strength to protest against sexual violence.

Yet the notion of women's sexuality as property was also embedded in the language, further hampering women's ability to protest.[13] The public discourses about rape distorted the reality of women's experiences; by making women ashamed to speak about sexual matters and by claiming the power to define sexual assault as an expert preserve, legal and medical discourses repressed women's ability to define rape and protest against it. These discourses structured the definition of rape around oppositions of chastity and unchastity, so that a rapist would only be punished if he assaulted a chaste woman. They regarded the distinction between rape and seduction as unimportant; a woman was damaged property in either case. From a woman's point of view, different dichotomies structured the definition of rape: the opposition of pleasure and pain, desire and repugnance, consent and rejection.

Women always viewed rape as a physically painful attack, yet the trauma of not being able to find the words with which to explain their feelings compounded women's anguish. The contrast between the public myth of rape and the private terror, the notion of women's sexuality as property, and male indifference to women's consent, all blocked women's efforts to articulate rape as a crime committed against them. Furthermore, when women did protest during the early nineteenth century, newspapers and judges censored their words, for respectable women were not supposed to know of or speak about any sexual matter. Women then and now felt ashamed after rape, as if they, rather than their assailants, were the criminals. What society defined as seduction may have been forcible sex against a woman's consent, but she could not find the words to define it as rape.

Today feminists work to give women the words to express their anger, developing a new feminine vernacular with such words as 'date-rape' for attacks which nineteenth-century men would have defined as seduction. The period 1770 to 1845, in contrast, witnessed masculine attempts to narrow the definition of rape according to patriarchal criteria, as I will demonstrate in Chapter 4. They were obsessed with penetration by the penis and ejaculation, but for women, sexual assault which does not involve vaginal penetration can be as traumatic as rape, and when I refer to rape I am incorporating this fact into my analysis.

Today, feminists have also brought the sexual abuse of girls into public attention. Women's concern with this issue is not new, for as I show in Chapter 3, mothers sometimes violently retaliated against the molesters of their children. In fact, popular revulsion against the crime extended to the courts, which punished the rape of children (then defined as girls of twelve years and under) much more severely than they do today. Yet the abhorrence of child molesting paradoxically excused the rape of adult women as less harmful.[14] Legally, a child's consent was irrelevant to this crime, but for women, the issue of consent was of central importance.

Some contemporary feminists now argue that women's consent to heterosexual sex is always coerced, and define rape as one end of an oppressive continuum of heterosexual sex. It is true that many women in the period 1770 to 1845 'consented' to sex out of economic necessity, for fear of losing their jobs, needed to get married in order to survive, or to earn money through prostitution. Furthermore, heterosexual desire is socially constructed to encourage women's consent.

Catherine MacKinnon even claims that 'if sex is something men do to women, the issue is less whether there was force and more whether consent is a meaningful concept.'[15] But to state that women's consent is extracted through the eroticization of dominance, as MacKinnon does, ignores the multifarious means by which the laws and economic factors oppress women, and the ways ideology coaxes women into acquiescence.

To understand women as historical actors as well as victims, we must focus on consent. A woman could experience rape, prostitution, and love affairs quite differently: the first as a violent assault over which she had no control; the second, a degrading activity which enabled her to survive economically; and the last, the possibility of immediate pleasure and future pregnancy. Although prostitution and rape both result from the patriarchal notion of women's sexuality as property, the former allowed women a little more room to manipulate, to struggle to survive.

And women's consent was not always coerced. Women could consent out of desire during this period, for working-class customs allowed a woman to engage in premarital sex and still be considered respectable. The poor often preferred cohabitation to legal marriage. By diminishing the importance of women's consent MacKinnon evades this historical reality and does not acknowledge the fact that rape is diametrically opposed to desire.

Furthermore, it is necessary to focus on women's experience of consent or refusal precisely because nineteenth-century contemporaries ignored this distinction. Because women's status as sexual property was so important, it was not thought to be relevant whether rape, prostitution, or sexual desire led to the loss of female chastity. Judges and juries defined a woman's consent by her character, not by her own desire or discourse.

Historical background

The invention of the myth of rape as warning, and the suppression of women's speech about sex, must be understood in the context of the great changes which took place between 1770 and 1845. This era witnessed the formation of new class politics, especially the rise of the middle class; intensification of the notion of women's sexuality as property; and the response of the working class.

During this era, the middle class began to claim cultural, economic, and political power. Growing numbers of merchants, doctors, industrialists, manufacturers, tradesmen, lawyers, large farmers, and clerks swelled its ranks. As Leonore Davidoff and Catherine Hall have written, the middle class developed its identity not only through capitalist economics but also through 'separate spheres'. In the public sphere, men competed for economic and political power while in the private sphere of domesticity, dependent women provided a warm, loving home. The increasing separation of home life from business meant that the association of middle-class women with the domestic sphere enabled 'their sexuality and labour power [to] be contained . . . their personal behaviour used in pursuit of respectability and thus demonstratable financial worthiness', as Davidoff and Hall note. Propagandists for sexual purity and domesticity often wrote specifically to combat the challenge posed by Mary Wollstonecraft and later Owenite feminists to the restrictions of marriage.[16] Evangelicals celebrated chastity as the mark of a woman's virtue while newly professionalized doctors defined unchaste women as medically and morally deviant. The virtues separate spheres engendered enabled the middle class to assert moral superiority over the corrupt and profligate aristocracy, bolstering their own claims to political power.

The ideology of separate spheres also aided middle-class efforts to enforce the values of the work ethic and sexual puritanism on the labouring poor. Since the early eighteenth century, reformers had attempted to impose moral discipline on working people, prohibiting any amusements on Sundays, closing down fairs and regulating beerhouses in order to shape a sober, God-fearing, and above all hard-working populace. Evangelicals tried to move the amusements of the poor from pubs and streets to the home and church. Meanwhile, legal reformers, frustrated by the harsh criminal codes' inability to deter widespread theft and violence, turned from punishment to regulation in order to control the working class. The bobby on the beat – put in place by Sir Robert Peel's New Police Act in 1828 – seemed to prevent crime more effectively than the fear of capital punishment. If the city missionary could not persuade the poor to abandon the streets for the churches, policemen could prohibit gambling, ballad-singing, and political meetings.

Malthusian and Utilitarian discourses provided the 'scientific' basis for the claim that the poor were morally responsible for their plight. Unless the poor stopped marrying and reproducing, Malthus predicted in 1798, population would inexorably increase beyond the limits of the food supply to maintain it. The 'iron law of wages', claimed economists, rendered poor relief and trade unions useless in improving workers' conditions. Meanwhile, the boom and bust cycle of capitalist industry, and a rapidly expanding population, demanded some solution to the problem of poverty. In response, the 1834 New Poor Law permitted poor relief only in prison-like workhouses, and centralized its administration to avoid the paternalism which supposedly encouraged poverty.

All these means of regulating working-class behaviour severely affected women, for the suppression of female sexuality was often identified as the key to solving the problem of public moral order. Policemen and Evangelicals agreed upon the necessity of ridding the streets of 'abandoned women', but in the process they often restricted the freedom of all women. The promulgators of the New Poor Law attributed the burgeoning pauper population to the supposed immorality of poor women: as the solution, they formulated the infamous bastardy clauses which freed men from their previous responsibility for maintaining their bastard children, forcing poor unmarried mothers to go into the workhouse or starve. This harsh view of poor women's morality was not universal: officials of some charities regarded unmarried mothers as 'seduced maidens', victims of heartless libertines. However, they tended to define rape victims, common-law wives, poor unmarried mothers, and prostitutes alike, as fallen women who should repent for their sins.

This bourgeois moral offensive elicited a complex response from the working class, which was at this time forging its own political identity. Since the 1790s radicals had been criticizing the monarchy and aristocracy for their corruption and oppressiveness. Their intertwined struggles for political and economic rights, marked by Peterloo and Luddism, the National Union of the Working Classes, and the anti-Poor Law movement, culminated in Chartism. Working people also wished to safeguard their traditional freedoms and amusements: the lively fairs, the vigorous pub culture, the ginshops and street life of ballad singers and costermongers so reviled by moralists. Many radicals, however, viewed such amusements as detrimental to class consciousness; they desired to impart self-respect to working people, rejecting heavy drinking and relaxed sexual morals as robbing time and energy best devoted to the home, unions, and politics. They contrasted working-class virtue to upper-class decadence. Drawing on eighteenth-century bourgeois radical criticisms of aristocratic profligacy, nineteenth-century working-class radicals portrayed England's elites as sexually immoral and therefore unfit to rule. In 1820, King George IV's efforts to divorce Queen Caroline for adultery sparked widespread protests at his hypocrisy, for he was a notorious libertine, and fuelled criticisms of the monarchical principal itself.[17]

The radical focus on moral concerns also stemmed from the 'sexual crisis' faced by working people in the early nineteenth century.[18] Plebeian courtship customs, allowing a solemn promise of marriage to justify premarital sex, cohabitation without legal marriage, and folk methods of divorce such as wife-selling persisted throughout the mid-nineteenth century. Yet working people could not merely defend idyllic plebeian customs from moralistic middle-class regulations. An enormous, disturbing upheaval in gender relations accompanied the transformation of the masses of working people – the artisans, small shopkeepers, labourers, laundresses, needlewomen, servants, and sailors of the eighteenth century – into a working class of wage earners. In the North of England, production moved out of the home and small workshops into large, alienating factories. The enclosure movement, agricultural depression, and capitalist farming methods impoverished labourers who previously had at least a small plot of land or were provided room and board by their employers. Depression and deskilling deprived London artisans of pride in their craft and their prosperous standard of living. Most of all, the Napoleonic Wars (1798–1815) and subsequent economic slumps caused cyclical unemployment, exacerbated by the cruelties of the New Poor Law after 1834.

These factors undermined male workers' ability to marry, precisely when marriage became increasingly necessary for working women's survival. Many women were thus abandoned by their men who left them with illegitimate children and no means of support. The competition between low-waged female workers and skilled craftsmen exacerbated sexual antagonism when weaving, tailoring, and shoe-binding moved into sweated workshops or factories.[19] At the same time, the radical quest for self-respect and the middle-class ideology of separate spheres both posited an almost unattainable ideal of domesticity for working people. As it became more and more impossible for men to maintain their wives at home, domestic propagandists denigrated the wage-labour of wives. As skilled craftsmen refused to marry, moralists castigated the unmarried mother as a fallen woman.

One solution to this clash between heightened ideals and a decaying reality was to blame the upper classes for sexual disruption. The image of the aristocratic libertine seducing the poor village maiden served as a powerful symbol of the exploitation of the poor by the rich. Derived from eighteenth-century Jacobin novelists, such as Thomas Holcroft and Robert Bage, this image enlivened the penny-issue novels, ballads and melodramas which appealed to early nineteenth-century working people.[20] Radicals then drew upon the aristocratic libertine, thus a familiar fictional character, to add an emotive motif to the denunciations of upper-class perfidy in their political rhetoric.

This image countered middle-class portrayals of working people as sexually profligate. Instead of the rough and rude female labourers described by disapproving clergymen, women workers could be seen as fragile victims of class exploitation. It was especially useful as an image in the struggles over the bastardy clauses, for the Poor Law's promulgators depicted paupers as an animalistic mass of men and women procreating without restraint, and unmarried mothers as pauper seductresses who falsely accused rich men of fathering their bastard children. Placing the blame for the supposed immorality of millgirls on the shoulders of factory masters enabled radicals to restore the self-respect of working people under attack by bourgeois moralists.

The myth of the seduced maiden, however, did not help women who were raped or seduced to articulate their experiences. First, it rarely differentiated between the victims of rape and women abandoned by their lovers when pregnant; both were pitied, but neither understood. Rape was a violent attack, while illegitimacy usually resulted from courtships gone wrong. Second, the myth excused working-class men from culpability for their violence against women. Male employers did capitalize on their class power to exploit sexually the factory girls and domestic servants who laboured for them. But most victims of rape were attacked by men of their own class: fellow servants, carpenters, groups of young weavers who attacked country girls, even the men who courted them.

re channelling antagonism?

Sources

The reality of women's experiences of sexual assault is difficult to uncover, for the vast majority of rapes, even more then than now, were never reported to the authorities. Those women who did attempt to prosecute were exceptional in their bravery, anger, and ability to articulate their experiences. This book does not pretend to present a complete or representative account of the totality of sexual assault experienced by women between 1770 and 1845, but I believe it is important to use the evidence that we do have, for the alternative is to leave these women's voices silenced.

My conclusions are based on more than one thousand cases of sexual assault; because they come from several sources, however, a statistical analysis of the totality of cases is not feasible. When statistics derived from the various samples are given, they should not be taken as an attempt to depict 'scientifically' the reality of sexual assault for all women; instead, they are a way of understanding the evidence that is available. I have focused on London and the Northeast of England, mostly the county of Yorkshire, in order to contrast urban and rural contexts of sexual assault.

There is one unique source which reveals the experience of women who did not report rape to magistrates or the police: it is the archive of a London charitable institution which took in the illegitimate children of unmarried mothers. In order to discern if women were the proper objects of its benevolence, officials required petitioners to recount the circumstances of their seductions. Sampling one in three petitions from 1815 to 1845, I found that 190, or 18 per cent, reported that they had been raped. The validity of this source will be discussed in greater depth in Chapter 5. The accounts of these women – victimized most often by men they knew, especially men who courted them – provide insight into the vast number of rapes which occurred in everyday life, and compensate somewhat for the biases of newspapers and court records.

Eighteenth-century newspapers rarely reported rapes, and when they did, provided little useful detail. Fortunately, extensive court records exist for this period. I have examined depositions from 165 rape cases from 1770 to 1829 in the assize records of the North-east circuit (Yorkshire, Cumberland, Westmoreland, Northumberland, and Newcastle) in the Public Record Office, Chancery Lane. When a woman who had been raped wished to charge her assailant, she would go before a magistrate who would take down her account as a sworn deposition. Depositions were also taken from the accused man or men and witnesses. The magistrates then sent these depositions to the clerk of the assizes (the crown court which met two or three times a year in each major county centre). The assize minute books and local newspapers indicate the outcome of these cases. These depositions are an extremely rich source: they contain not only factual information about occupations of assailants and victims and the circumstances of attacks, but also the emotional reactions of victims and witnesses. Many of these depositions never resulted in a trial; this fact reveals the disparity between the seriousness with which victims regarded rape, and the common refusal of magistrates and grand juries to prosecute their assailants.

No rape depositions survive in the assize records after 1829. To continue my analysis of rape in Yorkshire, I have also examined 160 cases of sexual assault reported in local newspapers (the *Leeds Intelligencer*, the *Leeds Mercury*, and the *Northern Star*) for the crucial period 1830 to 1845, a time when adult women began to work in factories in large numbers and political agitation convulsed the area. These newspapers contain reports of sexual violence brought before magistrates at petty sessions or quarter sessions as well as trials at the assizes.

Most London rape cases were tried at the Old Bailey; they were reported in the printed transcripts of all its criminal trials, including fifty-one rape cases for the period 1770 to 1796. These transcripts revealed women's detailed testimony about sexual attacks and also evidence of the scornful manner in which judges treated women. To supplement the Old Bailey records, I have examined the surviving magistrates' minute books from 1780 to 1796 and 1801 to 1803 which contain brief notes on twenty-one sexual assault cases which never came to trial. There are also 191 indictments and recognizances for attempted rape in the Middlesex Sessions papers (London area quarter sessions) which only provide details of name and occupation as well as conviction rates.

For the early nineteenth century it is much more difficult to find direct testimony from London women about rape. From 1796, the Old Bailey Court began to suppress the • publication of transcripts of sexual crimes, chiefly rape and sodomy; presumably, judges wished to protect the public from exposure to such 'offensive' testimony. The suppression of 'immorality', however, has always served to obstruct women's voices and conceal their oppression, for their ability to speak out against crimes committed against them was also suppressed. To examine rape in nineteenth-century London, I have therefore been forced to rely on newspaper reports of sexual assault cases in magistrates' courts and quarter sessions.

The popularity of newspapers greatly increased during the first few decades of the nineteenth century, partially due to their vastly expanded coverage of criminal trials. I have collected 238 cases of sexual assault through sampling three months of every year of the *Sun* from 1800 to 1815, from every year of *The Times* from 1815 to 1845, and from every other year of the *Weekly Dispatch* from 1815 to 1845. The *Sun* was a conservative daily. *The Times*, then as now, was the established paper of the middle and upper classes, yet its coverage of crime was lurid and detailed. In cases of sexual assault, it was more likely to impugn a victim's respectability if she was of plebeian origin. The *Weekly Dispatch* was the most popular newspaper in England in the 1830s and 1840s as its radical sympathies and detailed police-court coverage attracted a large working-class audience.[21] Cases from various radical and unstamped newspapers of the 1830s and 1840s augment these periodicals.

Newspapers, however, reported only about a quarter of the incidents of sexual assault known to the authorities, and did not of course provide a representative sample of such cases. Their accounts cannot be taken as an accurate portrayal of the experience of victims of sexual assault, for they should be seen as ideological sources whose stories were shaped by patriarchal and middle-class values. Nonetheless, they do have a certain usefulness. By comparing the reports in various newspapers their biases and accuracy can be assessed. My use of reports of sexual assaults from these newspapers is based on two assumptions: first, that incidents reported from police courts and assizes did happen and thus reflect some indication of the danger of sexual attack faced by women; and second, the ideological biases of newspaper accounts reveal the ideological construction of the fear of rape.

Newspaper accounts emphasized the degree to which a victim's behaviour made her culpable and rarely conveyed the physical trauma of rape, using euphemisms such as 'shameful outrage' to describe indecent exposure and gang rape alike. The middle-class myth of rape as a warning to women could be propagated most effectively through newsprint. Although newspapers were expensive, with the notable exception of illegal 'unstamped' radical journals, working people could peruse them in pubs and coffeehouses, where they were also read aloud to customers. Since the poor were sometimes taught how to read and not write, the proportion of those who could read in the 1830s and 1840s has been estimated at between two-thirds and three-quarters of the working class. About 51 per cent of women could sign their names in 1841.[22]

Another source for attitudes about rape is popular literature. Even those who were illiterate could hear ballads sung on the streets or in pubs. Ballads originated in oral folk culture but by the late eighteenth and early nineteenth centuries they also provided the basis for a flourishing commercial industry. Pamphlets about lurid crimes and 'last dying speeches' of executed criminals were also sold by balladsellers, who would reel out every gory detail in an effort to entice customers.[23] Many of these tales contained explicit moral messages to young men and women. While tragic songs about aristocratic libertines and seduced maidens obviously bore little resemblance to most working people's lives, comic ballads gained their humour by exaggerating commonplace behaviour.

Rape also featured prominently in literature written for a more genteel audience: the three-decker novels of the eighteenth century. In Eliza Haywood's *The History of Miss Betsy Thoughtless* (1751), for instance, the eponymous heroine repeatedly finds herself in danger from libertines due to her own foolishness. Richardson's Pamela fights off sexual attacks from her master so valiantly that he marries her. However, this book will not discuss such novels in detail, for it is unclear if they have any relevance to women's actual experience of rape, especially for working women. By the early nineteenth century, penny-issue novels appealing to working women began to appear, featuring melodramatic plots of aristocratic libertines seducing innocent village maidens. As my article 'The Politics of Seduction' (in *The Progress of Romance*, edited by Jean Radford, Routledge & Kegan Paul, 1986) reveals, this theme conveyed a political message while concealing the reality of rape within the working class.

Legal texts, guides to medical jurisprudence and charitable publications also reveal the attitudes of authorities who had so much power over working women. This book, however, is intended to allow the voices of rape victims to come through as strongly as the discourses of the male authorities who silenced them. It begins by contrasting women's experience of the pain and shame of rape with the masculine libertinism of the eighteenth century in Chapter 2; Chapter 3 discusses the indifference of the eighteenth-century justice system toward rape. Chapter 4 shows how this indifference gave way to a chivalrous protection which actually constrained women's behaviour even more, while Chapter 5 contrasts the melo-dramatic image of the seduced maiden with the reality of working-class courtship. Chapter 6 goes beyond radical rhetoric to show how the Industrial Revolution had only a limited impact on women's vulnerability to sexual violence, and Chapter 7 points out that the early nineteenth century witnessed the growing influence of the myth of rape as warning. Finally, Chapter 8 applies historical conclusions to feminist analyses of rape today.

CHAPTER 2

Women's pain, men's pleasure: rape in the late eighteenth century

The late eighteenth century was an era when sexual mores were fluid. While languishing young wives read bourgeois novels which warned them to protect their chastity as their most precious jewel, great ladies of the court openly engaged in illicit affairs and illegitimate ménages, relying on their wealth to protect them from scandal. The rape of Clarissa, Richardson's beautiful middle-class heroine, absorbed his readers for fourteen volumes, but the everyday rapes of labouring women stirred little sympathy.

For the lives of these women dramatically differed from the elegant scenes of elite affairs: they flirted, fought, and drank in the streets, ran stalls in fishmarkets, and carried vegetables to Covent Garden Market; they sold themselves in alleys or high class brothels, or lived with men with or without the bourgeois bonds of legal marriage. Labouring women faced many contradictions in this turbulent, dangerous and bawdy world. Their strength moved heavy loads but brought low wages; their sexuality was celebrated in ballads but denigrated by the upper classes; their safety protected by their own bravery but endangered by the violence they faced every day. Stern magistrates judged their behaviour as immoral, even as these jurists profited from prostitutes' payoffs.[1]

Such contradictions in Georgian sexual mores shaped both female and male responses to rape: a working woman may not have valued chastity as the measure of her self-worth, but if she were violated, others would regard her as damaged property. For some men, the low value placed on the chastity of poor women, and public indifference to their fate, may have encouraged a libertinism which excused rape. These responses turned on the eighteenth-century tendency to express the 'value' of female sexuality in brutally economic terms. Contemporary slang incarnated the notion of a woman's sexuality as property, defining female genitals as 'commodity', 'purse', or 'ware',[2] while bourgeois language was more genteel, referring to chastity as a woman's 'treasure' or 'jewel'. These words describe a 'sexual economy': the ways in which sexuality is affected by economic relations between men and women.

But the status of female sexuality as property was not universal in eighteenth-century England. Some women could earn a living for themselves and their children, so they would not necessarily have to regard their sexuality as property. Instead, they possibly conceived of it as a capacity for pleasure. However, where women could not subsist on their own, they were forced to regard their sexuality as an economic resource: marriage became a means of subsistence for women as well as or instead of a productive partnership or a source of companionship.

The very fluidity of the eighteenth-century sexual economy affected women's reactions to rape. Working women faced a confusing assessment of their worth: as workers or as sexual beings. For some, their ability to earn wages and do heavy work may have enabled them to protest more vigorously against rape, but magistrates and neighbours still judged them by patriarchal criteria and imparted a sense of shame. Religion reinforced the importance of female purity for upper- and middle-class women, who often came to regard their self-worth as defined by purity and sexlessness, but this was not necessarily true of working women. For many poor women, rape may have been just one of many experiences of sexual exploitation and male violence in a time when they often had to sell their sexuality for subsistence. In her novel, *Maria, or the Wrongs of Women* (1798), Mary Wollstonecraft vividly depicted the way sexual exploitation shaped working women's survival as she related the story of Jemima, the illegitimate daughter of a groom and a maidservant who died in childbirth. Jemima was sent out as a young girl to serve in a slop shop; there, her master, 'by blows and menaces, compelled me to submit to his ferocious desire', and when she became pregnant, her mistress threw her out into the streets. After trying to earn a living as a laundress, working impossibly long hours with her hands in freezing water, she turned to prostitution and eventually became the kept mistress of a wealthy, cultured man who educated her. When he died, however, she lost the status she had gained and was reduced to servitude once more. Embittered by her sordid story, she told the narrator, 'I have since read in novels of the blandishments of seduction, but I had not even the pleasure of being enticed into vice.'[3]

The sexual economy also shaped masculine responses to rape. Men of all classes could afford to be the buyers rather than the sellers of sexual property; the worth of men was not defined by their chastity. In fact the opposite was often true. Of course, there existed a large body of opinion advocating a Puritanical self-control for men, especially of the middle classes, but the libertines, even if a minority, strongly influenced attitudes toward rape. The eighteenth-century hero was often a rake: an aristocrat who spent his considerable resources on luxuries, rather than hoarding them in a 'spermatic economy' as the nineteenth-century industrialist would do. The Victorian ideal of patriarchal manliness, which expected men to protect their women from economic want and physical danger, was not yet prevalent; more often, libertines boasted of stealing other men's women. If a woman did not behave in a 'chaste' manner, some men regarded her as fair prey. Although many enlightenment thinkers acknowledged female sexuality and advocated a relaxed, pleasure-seeking eroticism, much libertine literature celebrated the heroic rapist and excused men's abandonment to their 'uncontrollable' passions.[4] Popular culture contained a misogynist, sexually violent streak which mirrored upper-class libertinism; for instance, contemporary slang had many violent words for sex but none for rape. An eighteenth-century *Dictionary of the Vulgar Tongue* defined 'knock' as 'to copulate' and 'to knock under' as 'to submit'; 'to wap' could mean either 'to copulate' or 'to beat'.[5]

In fact, women and men seem to have inhabited different universes with regard to rape. The definition of rape was culturally constructed, but it was publically constructed by and for men. For men, rape was a crime only if the victim could be seen as chaste, i.e. the property of another man; if not, the rapist felt he was exercising his right to 'take' any woman. For women, the definition of rape was engraved on their minds by lack of consent, and on their bodies by physical pain which no amount of cultural conditioning could soothe.

Women and the eighteenth-century sexual economy

The presence of women in public space was taken for granted in the eighteenth century, and their labours in factories and fields fuelled the economy. Though they enjoyed more freedom to move about in public space than their Victorian sisters were to experience, they still faced the danger of rape wherever they lived, worked and played. Rape was an arbitrary terror which afflicted a woman no matter how she behaved.

In the North-east, women worked mainly in agriculture and textiles, as the population was a mixture of small artisanal households and farmholdings, and larger farms and workshops. The prevalence of the independent female labourer characterized many areas in the transition from small farming to capitalist agriculture; women were needed as day labourers on large farms, and Victorian taboos on heavy work for women had not yet come into being. Many women day labourers earned relatively good wages for the heavy labour they performed. In some areas, women did the reaping; they travelled alone throughout the country to work in the harvest, and at other times of the year they tended turnip and potato fields. They scaled fields and pulled rocks from the roads.[6]

However, when they were working alone in the fields, they were vulnerable to attacks from men travelling through the area – that is, from men strong enough to overcome these muscular women's resistance. In the North-east assize records, 43 per cent of rapists chose victims who were travelling across the lonely moors or through fields, typically from home to work. Twenty-two per cent of the rapists found their victims working alone in fields. As one assailant told his victim in a Whitby pasture, 'No one but the ships will hear your screams.'[7] Yorkshire women were renowned for their brute strength; the assize records reveal that rapists often found it difficult to overcome their victims. Anataxeros Harper struggled for nearly two hours with Mary Harper before he succeeded in his self-declared goal of 'taking her Maidenhead'.[8]

Women who worked indoors, however, were not safe from rapists either. Eighteen per cent of the rapists came to their victims' homes and found them alone there; 10 per cent of rapes were committed in houses by masters, lodgers, or fellow servants. Service, of course, was the major female occupation. Seven per cent of the depositions did not indicate the location of the rape.

Although a rapist could more easily assault a woman working alone, the location of women's work obviously did not determine whether she would be raped or not; the point is that rapists could be found anywhere in ordinary life. However, women's work may have helped shape their self-images, and therefore the possibilities for reacting to rape. Working away from the patriarchal home did not necessarily gain women complete economic independence; their wages were still lower than men's. Yet the heavy work and relatively high wages of field workers, and the gains of women weavers during the domestic textile industry boom of 1770 to 1800, must have given them strength and self-confidence.

And there is some evidence that women enjoyed more sexual freedom in these locales. While the Methodists were influential in this area, their message of self-control still only reached a minority. Traditionally, country people accepted premarital pregnancy; couples courted in fields or even in their homes while parents slept. In the heyday of domestic industry, when both husband and wife could work as weavers, the marriage age dropped as young men and women saw no point in restraining their sexuality; it is possible more egalitarian sexual relations resulted.[9]

Several popular Northern ballads affirmed the connection between a woman's independent, productive work and her active, indeed insatiable sexuality. A Newcastle song, 'The Threshing Machine', tells the story of a handsome young farmer who euphemistically asks his maid Molly to work the threshing machine with him. While his 'Dobbin' soon becomes thin and lean, in nine months Molly produces 'the fruits of her labour, a young threshing machine'.[10] In another Newcastle ballad, a dairy maid sings, 'in minding my dairy I take great delight,/ in making of butter and cheese that is new,/ And a young man to play on my how-de-do.' Despite her mother's warning, she declares,

> For all her advice I care not a fig,
> For young men shall play with my hairy wig . . .
> My snatch is my own, the ground is the King's.
> It is free for a young man that brings a good thing,
> Let him be ever so strong or ever so stout
> I'll warrant I'll make him quickly give out.[11]

If a woman did have such a view of sexuality, she might regard rape as a violent assault which deprived her of the right to desire or refuse a sexual encounter, and which violated her right to regard her sexuality as a source of pleasure rather than pain.

In fact, North-east women did not express any feelings of shame in their assize depositions during the eighteenth century, while in the London Old Bailey trial records, 14 per cent of the rape victims explicitly stated they felt rape had brought shame upon them. Mary Currell, the daughter of a ropemaker, said she felt reluctant to mention the rape before two men she didn't know, or even her own father.[12] Mrs Ann Clarke did not tell the man she lived with or the female lodger who nursed her the true cause of her terrible injuries for several days after she lay ill, 'on account of shame'.[13] The difference may partially stem from the circumstances in which these women recounted their experience: the Old Bailey courtroom was crowded and imposing, while women in the North-east gave their depositions before a single magistrate, usually in his own home. London women were also less likely to tell male friends or relatives about rape than were women in the North-east.

Women in the metropolitan culture of London faced sharp contradictions in prevalent views of their sexuality and its place in the sexual economy. On the one hand, whether daughters, wives, or without family, all but prosperous women were expected to help maintain themselves and their children, but on the other, they often had to regard their sexuality as a resource for survival. Some women engaged in skilled craft work or employed other women in the trades of upholstery, mantua making, millinery, or weaving. Many wives ran their own shops or helped in their husbands' trades, while young unmarried women generally worked as servants. Skilled artisans often enjoyed prosperity and comfort in late eighteenth-century London, but the vagaries of trade could quickly plunge them into penury. As Dorothy George noted, the insecurity of London life affected women most severely; they performed the most low-paid, tedious, and heavy labour.[14]

Like women of the North-east, eighteenth-century London women enjoyed greater sexual freedom than Victorian mores were to allow them. In his memoirs Francis Place describes how the daughters of his artisan neighbours slept with several different men, unashamed of their illegitimate children.[15] For anyone below the respectable ranks of the middling classes, cohabitation was a common substitute for marriage, and marriage itself was rarely regarded as permanent.[16]

The economic insecurity of their position, however, often forced women to exchange their sexuality for subsistence. Middle- and upper-class women, of course, needed to safeguard their chastity for marriage unless they had independent incomes, and bourgeois thought defined any woman who had sex outside of legal marriage as a prostitute.[17] Not even marriage could guarantee the survival of working women. Prostitution was a major female occupation, ranging from kept mistresses to needleworkers who would occasionally pick up a man to streetwalkers who sold themselves in alleys for a shilling or two.

The conditions of London women's work are reflected in

the testimony from women in the Old Bailey trials as to who raped them and where. Since most young labouring women worked as apprentices or servants, it is not surprising that 18 per cent were raped by fellow workers or male servants and 20 per cent by their masters. Working alone in houses away from relatives and friends, they were particularly vulnerable to such assaults. Assailants had less opportunity to find women alone outdoors; only 25 per cent of the rapes occurred as women travelled on boats, through streets, in coaches, or in fields. Fifty-nine per cent of the victims were raped at home or in an indoor workplace. In 16 per cent of the cases, the rapist lured his victim to a strange house.

But there were more similarities than differences in the ways London and Yorkshire women reacted to the experience of rape. No matter how a woman regarded her sexuality, rape was a traumatic experience. If a woman prized her chastity as essential for marriage, a rapist ruined her. If she regarded her sexuality as a source of her own pleasure, the rapist violated her right to desire or refuse. If she sold her sexuality for subsistence, rape was still an unexpected, violent assault.

For all women, rape was and is an agonizing physical experience. Forcible penetration itself is painful, and the women who reported rapes in the eighteenth century were often physically harmed in other ways. It is possible that women who suffered additional violence beyond forcible penetration may have been more likely to report rape.[18] Seventy per cent of the victims of rape in the London court records stressed that the rape 'hurt' them, and many continued to be ill for a considerable time afterwards. Young virgins, respectable London matrons, and strong Yorkshire farm workers alike experienced this pain. A young lady named Ann Boss testified that her assailant 'was so violent he hurt me prodigiously . . . . I know I felt so ill I thought I was dying . . . .'[19] A witness described Mary Cunnill, a Yorkshire labourer who fought off her attacker, as 'so much hurt and ill-used that she was supported by three or four women, and looked almost dead from the ill-usage she received.'[20]

To avoid such pain and humiliation, women did all they could to resist rape, and often succeeded in fighting off their attackers. Given the heavy labour many women performed, their ability to defend themselves is not surprising. In fact, London women were notorious for fighting each other and even men in neighbourhood quarrels. For instance, Ann Hobbs, a London landlady, told a magistrate how she fought off the attack of her lodger: after he 'came into the bedroom he threw her down and attempted to be rude with her – she struggled for a long time and at length caught him by the Neckhandkerchief and almost choked him (sic).'[21]

Literature and song celebrated the woman who was able to protect her honour from an assailant. One popular ballad, 'The Bloomsbury Milkmaid', told the story of a woman courted by a squire; when he threatened to take her virginity by force, she stabbed him. The ballad reveals itself as fantasy when he recovers and, so impressed by her virtue, marries the milkmaid and makes her a rich lady.[22] Yet these praises of female fortitude implicitly slandered women who could not fight off rapists.

A rape victim's honour, no matter how she struggled, was thought to be irrevocably tarnished according to bourgeois values. In one famous rape case the prosecutor emphasized that while 'the injured lady may be as chaste as unsunned snow, she will never more be considered as immaculate.'[23] Eighteenth-century popular sex manuals were obsessed with proofs of virginity.[24] London husbands of rape victims sometimes, though not always, viewed rape as a justification for separating from their wives. Penelope Askew's husband, a painter of miniatures, declared that 'after such a heinous crime, and such a disagreeable affair, it was impossible ever to think of living with her'.[25] Elizabeth Stone's husband doubted her story of being raped by three neighbourhood boys; he told her 'if she did not prosecute the prisoners, and clear up her character, he would not live with her; for he would not be made a cuckold of by a one-eyed boy.'[26]

Given the shame of rape, women in both London and the North-east tended to use euphemisms to describe what happened to them: their most common term was 'ill-used'. 'Ill-used' effectively conveyed the pain and injury women felt from the general violence of the assault, but it also revealed women's reluctance to admit they had been raped, as the term was not synonymous with violation. For instance, servant Elizabeth Smithson told her sister, 'The Man had better taken her life, for that he had used her very ill more than once, and left it to her to know what she meant by such expressions.'[27] Mary Wilds, a sixteen-year-old London servant, reported to a watchman 'she had been ill-used, but did not mention particulars; she said she did not tell she had been ravished . . .'.[28]

Many victims seemed to regard rape as too shameful or private to tell men and hoped that their mothers, sisters, or even mistresses would be more sympathetic. For instance, after Elizabeth Wilson was raped by a soldier on an errand to the barracks, she waited until her mistress came home and then 'ran to her, threw her Arms around her neck, kissed her, and cried out, Mr. Quin has ruined me . . .'.[29] As soon as her assailant left her, Penelope Askew rushed to her sister, who urged her to prosecute the rapist.[30] Women were sometimes more ready to interfere when witnessing rapes. Although John Smith and Sarah Scott both saw a young girl being assaulted in Green Park, she moved more quickly to help; as she testified, 'the cries that I heard were shocking for any human species, almost, to bear it; I asked John Smith to go up; he rather refused it, and I went up myself, and immediately he followed me . . . . I asked [the assailant] if he was not a rascal.'[31]

When women hesitated before telling men about rape, their fears were often justified. Obertus Hamley closely questioned Mrs Mary Bradley when she told him Ralph Cutler had raped her, asking if there had been any previous intimacy between them.[32] After her uncle raped fifteen-year-old Ann Bradshaw on a North Riding moor, the men to whom she ran for aid merely asked, 'if he had made a whore of her'.[33]

Reactions to rape, however, could not be strictly divided on gender lines. Many lovers, husbands, and fathers were sympathetic to victims and furious at rapists, while the succour of other women could not be taken for granted. Some women learned all too well the harsh rules of the sexual economy of the late eighteenth century and judged other women by its criteria. Even while they pitied the victim of rape, they viewed her as culpable; they feared her taint would infect themselves, or that the assailants would turn on them. One cold December morning in 1780, for example, Mary Delvin and Mary Wilkinson heard Isabella Ray cry out, 'Ladies, ladies, have compassion on a woman!' and saw that two men were raping her in an alley. Mary Delvin moved to assist her, but Wilkinson and another man held her back, saying they would be served the same way themselves. Although Mary Wilkinson rebuked one of the assailants, shouting, 'd—n your blood, if you had served me so I would have hanged you if you had all the necks in the world', she then turned to the victim, inquiring, 'Are you not ashamed, such an old woman as you, to lie with so many fellows?'[34]

Women's reactions to rape must also be put in the context of the pervasive sexual exploitation of the eighteenth-century sexual economy. For many women, the exchange of their sexuality for subsistence was inevitable; rape was just one of many outrages, including widespread violence against women by their husbands, men in the neighbourhood, customers, and strangers, and the necessity of resorting to prostitution for survival. A few women refused to take rape victims seriously, urging them to seek cash rather than revenge from rapists. After Elizabeth Farrier, an orphan servant, was raped by a neighbour, her mistress just laughed and 'halled such jeers at me' (sic) and told her, 'Betty, do not look down, if he has got you with child, his long legs is able enough to keep it.' Elizabeth's aunt testified that the mistress told her the rapist 'was a man worth money . . . and that it was a pity to hang him.'[35]

Women occasionally told each other that violent sex was an unavoidable travail of female life. After fifteen-year-old Martha Linett was raped by a soldier, Ann Lock, who had introduced them, merely told her, 'It was what I must come to, and she must come to, and all women must come to.'[36]

Most disturbing of all, a few women profited by exploiting others in the sexual economy: during 1770 to 1780 five women were accused of aiding and abetting men who raped young girls.[37] In most of these cases, the woman enticed the young girl away from her mistress or mother, luring her to the home of a man who paid her for his victim; this was a coercive extension of the common practice of older women luring young girls into prostitution. The very rare questionable rape charges found in late eighteenth-century court records involved similar situations, in which girls voluntarily sold themselves, craving money and excitement, but changed their minds when they realized the physical pain involved. Thirteen-year-old Hannah Mordecai went willingly to a bawdy house with Mary Solomon, but her purchaser's pleasure pained her. Afterwards, she dried her tears when he gave her a guinea; she split the money with Mary Solomon and made no complaint until her parents discovered what happened.[38]

The only such case in the North-east assize record further illuminates women's feelings about prostitution and rape. Ann Greenwall, a servant, did not press charges against Newcastle gentleman Jonathan Thompson until the third time he had sex with her, and only then because a neighbour confronted her as she left the bawdy house of one Mrs Charlton. On her second examination before a magistrate, she revealed that Mrs Charlton had repeatedly solicited her to come to her house on a mysterious errand. When she finally came, the woman put her into a little room with a strange man, who with much difficulty persuaded her to have sex with him. He then gave Mrs Charlton eight shillings, half of which she gave to Ann. Apparently Ann's value decreased with time; after the third incident, the man gave her only one shilling. When her mistress reproached Hannah Charlton for using her servant so ill, she laughed 'and seemed to make a light matter of it . . . and said that he had also used the said Hannah Charlton's sister in the same way . . .'. Ann Greenwall pressed charges to save her reputation in the neighbourhood, but she also felt physically hurt and coerced into prostitution.[39] Perhaps she expected that selling herself would be more pleasurable (and lucrative) than it turned out to be.

However, the acceptance of women's sexuality as a 'commodity' (the slang word for female genitalia) did not mean that women accepted rape. Women who engaged in sexual commerce could still regard rape as an outrage. The notion that prostitutes cannot be raped, of course, stems from a patriarchal notion of a woman's consent as shaped by her relation to men rather than her own free will. The fact that many women who did not meet strict standards of chastity prosecuted their assailants indicates that they did not accept such a definition of consent.

For example, Mary Hunt, who cohabited with a lifeguards-man and had been accused of prostitution by the parish authorities, prosecuted a man who raped her on Brompton Road; for her, her way of life had nothing to do with the fact that she had been raped.[40] Even a streetwalker would sometimes successfully defend herself on the charge of theft from a customer by accusing him of assaulting her. For a prostitute, the fact that a man paid her meant he could only expect certain sexual acts, not the right to indiscriminately abuse her. Mary Jones, for instance, excused her theft from a foreigner by claiming he 'pulled me about on the bed, in a ridiculous manner; I never saw a man have such actions in my life.'[41] If a man 'stole' sex from a prostitute by refusing to pay her, she could rob and/or beat him in retaliation. Prostitutes, after all, wished to control their own bodies as much or even more than other women.

Libertinism and masculine attitudes toward rape

Men could react violently to women who insisted on a fair price for their sexuality, or refused to desire them. In a male-dominated society, men ultimately were the more powerful partners in every sexual transaction. In the eighteenth century as well as now, sexual freedom meant quite different things for men and women. While a woman may have sought sexual pleasure, a man did not necessarily acknowledge her right to desire or refuse. When a woman's economic position was tenuous, she could sell her sex in order to survive, while for a man, female sexuality became a 'commodity' to be bought, bartered for, or stolen by force.

The motivations of rapists must be understood in the context of the masculine place in the eighteenth-century sexual economy. Men of all classes could earn more money than women; they almost never needed to sell their sexuality to gain subsistence.[42] Instead, men could perceive their sexuality as a source of pleasure apart from procreation; furthermore, given their dominant economic, and social position, men had more power to win the object of their desires. As a violent, aggressive assault, rape was and is the extreme expression of a socially-constructed masculine sexuality in which men are supposed to be the active, dominant, partners. Rapists believed they had a right to 'take' any woman they wanted, as part of the masculine privilege as the dominant sex. When sex was regarded as the taking of a woman rather than a mutually pleasurable act, her desires faded in importance.

Both rape trials and popular literature reveal evidence of the belief that men's 'uncontrollable' passions caused rape. The Enlightenment elevation of 'nature' could buttress a libertine philosophy of pursuing pleasure at every turn. Manasseh Dawes, a London barrister who wrote on the criminal law, claimed that rape was the 'artless sincerity of natural passion.' In the rapist, Dawes went on, 'desire is whetted, importunity fails, passion increases, opportunity is favourable, and natural force is employed;' he blamed the female victim because 'her endearments alone excited' this violence.[43]

The 1786 trial of John Motherill perfectly illustrates the prevalence of libertine attitudes toward rape. One night in Brighton, a tailor named John Motherill encountered a young lady (as it turns out, a feeble-witted one) walking from a coach to her front door. He accosted her, seized her, dragged her to a churchyard and raped her repeatedly. As her family was prominent, he was soon brought to trial, and the case excited much public interest and sympathy; but he was found not guilty.

The libertine ethos predominated in the publicity surrounding the case, despite the efforts of the prosecuting counsel who tried to refute the influence of 'persons in the world who are apt, at first view, to consider that men are led to the commission of that crime by a natural appetite, and therefore to look at it with a less degree of horror . . .'[44] Sexual assault was a titillating and amusing subject for many men. Bage notes in his novel *Mount Henneth* that for certain young gentlemen, 'a trial for rape would have been an excellent pastime.'[45] In fact, scandalous rape trials provided titillating reading for literate wealthy men.[46] Motherill's trial was actually published with a semi-pornographic frontispiece, and he himself published a defense of his innocence in which he claimed that he took his victim for a prostitute and that she, persuaded by his charms, did not resist his advances.[47]

This licentious ephemera made Motherill into one of the eighteenth-century's 'heroic rapists', although admittedly he lacked the aristocratic cachet of his famed fellow violators, Colonel Francis Charteris and Frederick Calvert, Lord Baltimore. Nicknamed the Rape-master General, Charteris was notorious for repeated rapes of poor women, and it was reported that 'he brags he will sollicit for a Patent for ravishing where he pleases, in order to put a stop to all vexatious Suits which may interrupt him in his pleasures hereafter.'[48] In 1730 Charteris was found guilty of the rape of Ann Bond, his servant, but the King subsequently pardoned him. Lord Baltimore's exploits scandalized London society in the 1760s. He was known to keep 'seraglios' in his London and country houses; to augment them he kidnapped milliner Sarah Woodcock with the aid of several accomplices and raped her despite her desperate resistence, but he was acquitted of the crime. One of his defenders wrote that such a noble man would surely never need to use force; that rape was nearly impossible to commit, but when done, 'It is to be sure a lordly act.'[49]

While many libertines joined with one lord in declaring, 'he would not stick at anything to gratify his lust, except *Forcing* a woman against her inclination',[50] there is evidence that the heroic rapist influenced popular as well as elite libertine culture. Rapists bragged of their assaults, or did not bother to deny what was ostensibly a capital offense. Anataxerous Harper, caught in the act of raping Mary Wilson in a field, drunkenly declared to two witnesses, 'I have got a Maiden-head'; at his examination before a magistrate he merely claimed he had not succeeded in his goal of violating her virginity.[51] In London, after they had gang-raped Isabella Ray and left her to die of her injuries in the bitter cold, Frederick Thomas and Christopher Eyres 'bragged about what they had done to the woman'.[52] Six of fifty-one rapists tried at the Old Bailey were known to have boasted or at least carelessly admitted their assaults.

Accused rapists could even exploit their trials for rape as an opportunity to prove their virility. John Motherill asserted, 'I shall not be accused of vanity, when I declare that the people came in multitudes, from all quarters, to the sides of the roads through which we passed' on the way to his trial.[53] A pornographic journal, *The Ramblers' Magazine*, claimed that when Motherill was gaoled women flocked to him and proclaimed him a hero.[54] Lovelace, Richardson's fictional rapist, fantasized about white-gowned maidens celebrating his potency in the courtroom; in real life, James Dransfield, hung for rape and robbery, 'in passing to the place of execution . . . behaved in a most peculiar manner, by nodding and shaking his head to the women as he passed along the street, a smile on his countenance.'[55] Even after being pelted in the pillory for assaulting a ten-year-old girl, a man named Nelson 'took off his coat and gave three cheers' after being released.[56]

Libertines such as Motherill were so confident of their sexual prowess that they ignored women's resistance, portraying their victims' protests as coy acquiescence. To illustrate this more starkly, I will contrast the testimony of John Motherill with that of his victim, Catherine Wade.

In Motherill's version of events, he merely mistook her for a loose woman; as his editor notes, 'The conquest so easily obtained over the lady he (as so many others would have done in his situation) attributed to his own figure and address.' He claimed he met her on the street at midnight, proposed to take a walk, and then,

> finding her very conformable, I began to think I might proceed to any freedoms without giving offense, and

without any ceremony, took her around the neck and kissed her. I then placed my hand toward the upper part of her thigh (upon the outside of her Cloathes [sic]) when she cried out in an accent that did not express any displeasure, 'Oh fie! Do not do that here.'

Catherine Wade testified that Motherill pretend to be a servant with a message from her father.

He put his hand in my bosom, which I immediately pushed away; he said I was a very pretty girl, and kissed me. From such behaviour I was too terrified to speak. He now went to greater lengths, and impudently put his hand up my petticoats. I repulsed him, but in vain, for he only grew more daring and persevering.

She was somewhat feeble-witted and went into a state of shock as he assaulted her. In her story, he brutally raped her many times during the night; she came home, dirty, bruised, and almost insensible.[57]

Motherill's version of events triumphed, and his attitudes could be found far beyond elegant pamphlet literature in the oral culture of ordinary people. The popular notion that women had an insatiable sexuality may have excused rape, and bawdy songs often encouraged the myth that if a woman says no she really means yes. In the ballad 'The Answer,' Robin drives along a country road and offers a lift in his wagon to a young maiden passing by:

His Wagon he stop'd, and his leg o'er her laid.
Oh! What are you doing? then whisper'd the Maid,
She struggled, she threatened, she vow'ed she'd begone,
'Till fainter and fainter, she cry'd out, Drive on,
Drive on Robin, geeho, geeho.[58]

Sometimes men 'misinterpreted' women's refusal to consent and then raped them, while other men reacted violently to such refusals. There are many cases of men coming upon women in the streets or fields, asking for a kiss or cuddle, and assaulting women who rebuked them. These men apparently expected that women would desire such chance encounters –

or did not care what women desired. In 1796, for instance, William Brown accosted Ann Healey on the road to Saltwick and asked her, 'Will you have a sweetheart?' When she said no, he threw her down and said, 'You Bitch you lay still or I will cut your throat.' As she testified, he then 'ravished her in the most cruel manner.'[59] James Fenton, a 'gentleman', actually asked Elizabeth Brough if she had 'spent' (i.e. come to orgasm) after he violently raped her on the highway. She scornfully replied that he was 'a brute of a gentleman.'[60]

Some men seemed to consider that they had a right to molest women in the streets. John Williams and John Tailor, charged by Mrs Lucy Gill with taking her bundle and 'mauling' her, successfully escaped punishment for theft by claiming 'that they might molest her for anything they knew, but they had no thoughts in the world to take anything from her, and only attempted to kiss her.'[61] Magistrates' minute books reveal that indecent assaults on London streets were fairly common, although newspapers almost never reported them. For instance, in 1787 Sarah Hardy charged John Wright and Thomas Foster with 'the gross misconduct by insulting many women and particularly pushing one old Woman down by means of which she was so much hurt as to be in the Hospital.' They were committed to Bridewell as disorderly persons. In another incident, Thomas Gill testified that on crossing London Bridge 'I stopt to make water' when Benjamin Wall 'put his hand up my wife's petticoats and struck her on the breast'.[62] A lady calling herself 'Andromache' wrote to the *Universal Register* in 1785 that she had been brutally and indecently assaulted by a strange man on a crowded street and that no one came to her help.[63]

Although some men seemed to believe they had a right to rape, they did not just seize any available woman at whim; they planned their attacks, picking the most vulnerable women as their victims. Highwaymen sometimes sexually assaulted women as an afterthought to robbery. In Yorkshire, women were especially vulnerable as they travelled across the footpad-infested moors from one town to another. In 1796, Elizabeth Ayres was passing through Newcastle on her way to work in the harvest when she was approached by William

Johnson and two others, who cried out, 'Bugger your eyes you bitch where are you going?' After they took her meagre bundle, they attempted to rape her, but she escaped.[64]

Men sometimes offered women money for sex and robbed them when they refused. Edward Barry, for instance, was condemned to death for stealing a bundle from Sarah Ingram as she walked through some Bromley fields. According to Sarah, he offered her a shilling to come into a pasture with him, and grabbed her bundle when she turned him down.[65] Assailants excused robberies by claiming they had merely been trying to have sex with their victims. In Yorkshire, butcher Thomas Baxter denied he had violently raped Rachel Halliwell, a sailor's wife, and taken her bundle; in his version of events, she agreed to lie with him for a sixpence, but refused to give him change for a shilling, so he took her things in lieu of the money she purportedly owed him.[66]

As we have seen, the libertine ideology of both elite and popular culture presented rape as a 'natural' urge, merely the opportunistic use of violence to 'take' otherwise unavailable female sexuality. Manasseh Dawes even wrote (contrary to all available evidence) that only lower-class men raped because they could not purchase women's favours with either luxuries or cold cash.[67] But rape, which must be understood as a desire to dominate a woman with both sex and violence, must be put in the context of the many ways men dominated women in the late eighteenth century.

Rape is not only the forcible seizure of a woman's sexuality, it is a violent act aimed at humiliating women. Beyond the inherent violence of forcible penetration, 28 per cent of rapists in the Old Bailey records beat their victims, ranging from blows to severe assaults. Assailants seemed to wish to degrade the women they attacked, perhaps in part to justify the assault in their own minds by regarding the woman or child as an unworthy thing. They expressed hostility through swearing at their victims in 23 per cent of the London cases. A further 17 per cent hurt their victims by tearing their genitals with their hands, inflicting terrible injuries.[68] This violence may have been symptomatic of widespread misogyny in eighteenth-century London, and hints at the prevalence of sadistic sexual practices.

Men could sometimes use rape in order to reinforce women's subordinate position, and class doubled a man's power over a woman. Gentlemen could certainly rape poor women with impunity, as the cases of Lord Baltimore and Colonel Charteris, who committed multiple rapes and escaped punishment, reveal. However, most working women encountered few gentlemen in their everyday lives; they faced most danger from men of their own class (see Appendix I). Furthermore, middle- and upper-class rapists rarely fit the popular stereotype of the aristocratic libertine. In Yorkshire, such assailants included a comedian, a butcher, a clothier, a farmer, and a barber. In London, the masters accused of raping their servants included two publicans, a weaver, a brickmaker, a runner at the Shadwell Police Office, and one 'gentleman'.

And the class system incorporated a system of domination based on gender: men were disproportionately likely to be masters, and women to be servants. Women were less likely to be in the middling ranks on their own, simply because they were women and often excluded from skilled occupations. Girls were sometimes sent out as apprentices; if they were somewhat prosperous, to learn a trade such as millinery, or if they were paupers, as cheap labour for whomever would take them. Several London rape victims were tambour-work (embroidery) apprentices, a notoriously exploitative form of employment.[69]

But most young working women were domestic servants. While large aristocratic and bourgeois householders employed men as well as women, the young girls in these records were usually the only servants employed by weavers and shop-keepers, so the class status of a servant's parents would not necessarily be lower than that of her master.

Masters seemed to believe that they had a right to their servants' or apprentices' sexual favours, a right they would claim by force if servants did not acquiesce. Twenty-per cent of the Old Bailey rapes, and 9 per cent of the North-east assize cases, involved masters and servants. In 1772, when

Sarah Bishop, aged sixteen, claimed to her mistress that her master, publican George Carter, had raped her, she told her 'he always served all his servants so the night they came into the house'.[70] In this case, rape seems to have been almost a ritual assertion of the master's authority. The fact that William Hodge boasted before his London neighbours of raping his sixteen-year-old servant indicates he believed that he had committed no crime.[71]

The reason for the disparity between London and the North-east is not clear. It is possible that servants in the latter area were reluctant to prosecute their masters for rape, while metropolitan servants were notoriously insubordinate. In London, servants could easily obtain new employment, while in rural areas, a woman could be blacklisted and never find another place if she dared protest a rape.[72] The number of London female servants who prosecuted their masters for rape indicates that these women did not accept sexual services as their masters' right. Juries, however, did: no master was punished for rape in the eighteenth-century records I have examined.

Servants were especially easy prey because men of any class could take advantage of their youth and isolation within the household. London female servants were almost as vulnerable to rape from male servants and lodgers as from masters. Overall, men usually preyed on women of their own class, as can be seen from the nearly equal percentages of victims and rapists from the ranks of the labouring poor.

Class was not the only factor which gave men added power over women. Men also had the power of adulthood over girl children, for the class status of a little girl counted for little when faced with an assailant of greater age and physical strength. Servants sometimes raped their masters' daughters, reversing the usual stereotype of class exploitation. For instance, a publican charged James Craige, his potboy, with assaulting his ten-year-old daughter, and the servant of one of her mother's lodgers raped Cornelia Winter, only eight years old.[73] Daughters of publicans and lodging-house keepers were especially vulnerable to the men served by their parents, often men of the 'lower orders'.

Viewing sex as a thing to be taken, these men and boys found it easiest to take sex and exercise power over a small, weak child, who could not struggle and did not know how to protest. On the one hand, the rape of children by men was widely abhorred. In 1786, the *Universal Register* noted, 'The practise of committing the most shocking indecencies on children is quite common.'[74] On the other, some popular beliefs such as the myth that intercourse with a virgin would cure venereal disease exacerbated this problem. In 1752, fifty children were admitted to the Lock Hospital infected presumably by adults.[75] Such assaults inflicted terrible emotional and physical injuries on children, and their assailants were popularly detested and severely punished, regardless of the offender's status (as I will show in the next chapter). Perhaps the rape of children was thought to be unprocreative and therefore unnatural, as was sodomy, another 'crime' which excited great popular outrage. The child victims, however, did not escape the revulsion accorded to their assailants. A comment in the *Universal Register* called for charitable aid to 'those unfortunate children, who have been seduced or violated at the early age of ten or eleven, and thereby doomed through their future lives to rely on prostitution for subsistence.'[76]

In contrast, sexual violence committed by men on adult women tended to be seen as an extension of natural, everyday relations between the sexes, and thus much less culpable. The fact that rape in marriage was legal (as it still is today) underlines this point. Women could only protest against sexual violence committed by their husbands if it involved 'unnatural acts' (probably anal intercourse) or if the husband was violent, committed adultery with prostitutes, *and* infected his wife with venereal disease. Mary Bradshaw, wife of a Haines gardener, complained to a Justice that her husband not only beat her brutally, but 'has many times committed acts of indecency contrary to nature with her'.[77]

When Amelia Brazier, wife of a prosperous but 'debauched' wine vault keeper, refused to sleep with her husband, he beat her and tried to murder her. Fearful for her life, she took him before a London Justice but he 'impudently' declared 'he would beat and pox his wife whenever he thought proper'.[78] Despite the fact that many eighteenth-century wives contributed economically to their husbands' businesses, men always had the power of violence and rape over the women they married. Mary Emberson's dowry and bookkeeping skills allowed the illiterate Essex servant John Emberson to become a prosperous corn merchant, but he only showed his gratitude by abusing and beating her. When she refused to sleep with him and sought refuge with the servants, he dragged her from the room and kicked her on the thighs.[79]

Conclusion

Despite the literary attention paid to rape as a fictional motif, sexual abuse of working women excited very little public outcry. Labouring women only came to public attention as prostitutes: their public misery, and their perceived tendency to prey on respectable young men, excited calls for reformatories.

However, the public indifference toward the rape of working women also meant that rape was not used as a warning for working women to restrict their movements. In the nineteenth century, as today, rapes were often published as warnings to women to stay out of public space. However, there is little or no evidence for such warnings in court records, newspapers or popular literature of the late eighteenth century. The libertine pamphlet literature presented rape as titillating to men; because they were not aimed at women, they did not use rape to warn women to restrict their movements. For instance, the literature on Motherill did not question Catherine Wade's behaviour.

There are several reasons for this absence of such warnings. First, there was no clear consensus about how respectable women should behave. As we have seen, a strong Puritanical strain mandated timidity and chastity for middle-class wives and daughters, but some aristocratic ladies were well-known to live in less conventional arrangements. For many women of the labouring classes, premarital sex, common-law marriage, and serial monogamy were considered morally acceptable, and the streets were the centre of work and amusement.

Second, public discourses about rape were not addressed to the women who did traverse streets and fields. For middle-class women, gothic and sentimental novels expressed a constant fear of rape, but the attacks often took place within the home, inflicted by wicked guardians, fathers, uncles, lovers, masters, or suitors – *Clarissa* and *Pamela* are perfect examples.[80]

Third, newspapers did not use rapes as warnings to women to behave because they rarely reported rapes at all, preferring to concentrate on highway robberies of gentlemen. Eighteenth-century journalism, unlike its later counterpart, was not read by ordinary people.

However, women's behaviour was still controlled in many other ways. Middle-class women were warned that their chastity was the primary source of their virtue, to say nothing of their worth in the marriage market. Working women were often subordinated to the men they lived with or married because their wages were so much lower and because wife-beating was so common. Those working women who sold their sexual services on the street, or even women who simply wished to go out drinking or walking late at night, could be arrested as prostitutes and sent to their families or employers, if not to gaol.[81]

Rape was not publicized as a warning to women because so many men seemed to regard rape as a trivial issue, or of interest only as a source for amusing stories or scandal. Instead of expressing concern for rape as a serious crime, many men regarded it 'as a matter of prowess, and a subject of ridicule', as the prosecuting attorney in the Motherill trial noted.[82] There were exceptions: the Societies for the Suppression of Vice, popular among the middling ranks of tradesmen, encouraged male continence.[83] Their obsession with chastity, however, could serve to excuse the rape of women who did not meet their standards. Radicals did criticize aristocratic rapists and assailed the notion of female sexuality as property, but they were only a minority voice.[84] Neither reformers nor radicals could counteract the influence of the 'heroic rapist', or lessen the scorn with which rape victims' claims were greeted. The next chapter reveals how this scorn extended into the courts, which spared rapists but punished thieves according to the Bloody Code of eighteenth-century British justice.

CHAPTER 3

A public shame: rape and eighteenth-century justice

Eighteenth century British justice was overwhelmingly concerned with property: by the end of this era, over 200 crimes (largely minor thefts) could be punished by death. The law was ruthless in hanging teenage pickpockets, but its revenge rarely extended to rapists, although both had committed capital crimes.

The legal system served the interests of the propertied classes by ensuring the submissiveness of working people: its impressive machinery first elicited the fear of brutal punishment for minor crimes, then awe at the pomp and ceremony of the courts, and finally deference when powerful squires granted occasional mercy. As Douglas Hay and E.P. Thompson have shown, British justice helped prevent revolution through its ideology of equal rights: the people believed the law protected them as well as the rich, and radicals could sometimes manipulate the law to their own ends.[1]

Many women who had been sexually assaulted believed the law protected them too. They told their rapists they would gain revenge: Mrs Mary Bradley, the wife of an auctioneer, threatened Ralph Cutler 'he would certainly suffer for what he did', when he raped her, and Mrs Sarah Bethell warned a neighbour who assaulted her, 'Moody, I will expose you to everyone I know.'[2] In practice the ideology of rape as a serious crime was as deceptive as the ideology of equal rights: neither Cutler nor Moody was punished.

Women who attempted to gain redress by pursuing their assailants through the maze of the courts found their path fraught with difficulties. For in the eyes of the law sexual assault was only significant when it involved the 'property' of a man – a virginal daughter or wife. The law of rape, in fact, had evolved to protect the theft of female sexual property, not to protect women themselves. In medieval England, it was primarily formulated to deal with abduction and illicit marriage of heiresses.[3]

But rape was also punished by death because it was akin to murder: a woman's chastity defined her worth as a person, so without it, she herself was worthless. From this principle derived the expression that rape was worse than death; it was a kind of death.

This posed a paradox for legal practice. On the one hand, the rapist deserved to be punished because he had attacked female chastity, a valuable possession. On the other hand, the violated woman had lost her credibility as a prosecutrix along with her chastity. It is this paradox which accounts for the low conviction rate for rape: juries hesitated to hang a man for rape on the testimony of a woman who admitted publicly that she was unchaste and therefore unworthy.

Sexual assault, therefore, would only be punished if this paradox could be solved. Two solutions were possible; if the woman had fought off her attacker and preserved her chastity, prosecuting him only for attempted rape, or when a husband or father went to court to seek redress for his loss of property in a wife or daughter's chastity.

Juries more often convicted men accused of attempted rape than rape itself. While only 7 to 13 per cent of men accused of raping adult women were found guilty, juries convicted about a quarter of assailants accused of attempted violation.[4] A man accused of trying to violate a woman could be punished with a fine, or imprisonment ranging from a week to a year as well as the public humiliation of the pillory.

The contrast between the relatively high conviction rate for attempted rape and the very low conviction rate for completed rape cannot solely be attributed to the reluctance of juries to condemn a man to death. First, a woman who prosecuted for attempted rape declared publicly that she had risked her life defending her chastity, and that she should be believed because she was still chaste. But second, and more telling, is the fact that juries shed this reluctance when faced with men who had robbed the women they sexually assaulted. It was easier for a woman to get a man convicted to death for stealing her bundle worth a few shillings than to convince a jury he had raped her. Out of ten cases of trials for robbery which had involved indecent assault or rape, seven men were found guilty, and six condemned to death (although one was pardoned). In one case, Edward Barry offered thirteen-year-old Sarah Ingram a shilling, presumably to have sex with him, and when she refused, he took her bundle which contained 4s6d., a dish, and an apron. For this he was condemned to death.[5] Richard Etherington was also condemned to death for stealing clothes from Ann Hughes, a widow; they were old friends and had been drinking together one evening, when he attempted to 'get his ends of her' and 'used her ill'.[6]

Sexual assault would also be punished if the husband or father of the victim prosecuted her assailant. Eighteenth-century civil courts actively defended patriarchal honour, for husbands could sue their wives' lovers for 'criminal conversation'; fathers (or widowed mothers or brothers) could sue their daughters' seducers, ostensibly for loss of services. In both cases, juries usually awarded heavy damages to the plaintiffs.[7] Whether the daughter had been raped or consented to her seduction was completely irrelevant, although many such cases had actually involved sexual assault.

The criminal courts also consistently and severely punished sexual assaults on children; again, these cases were brought by the parents of the victim, and as we have seen in the last chapter, excited almost universal revulsion. In London, out of fifteen men tried in the Old Bailey Sessions between 1770 and 1799 for rape on girls under thirteen, five were found guilty and sentenced to death; four were remanded for trial on the charge of assault with intent to commit rape. Like men convicted of the 'unnatural crime' of attempted sodomy, men guilty of attempted rape were put in the pillory to face the rage of the populace. In one incident, 'a depraved wretch . . . stood one hour in the pillory in Great Russell Street . . . .

The concourse of women who had witnessed the hardened miscreant's shame was immense. They surrounded the pillory, and pelted him with filth and rotten eggs.'[8] In yet another case, a man put in the pillory almost died from the abuse.[9]

Although the sexual assault of children was thought to be much more unacceptable than the rape of adult women, many of these cases were never brought to court. Magistrate John Fielding blamed mothers for this, stating that 'offenders often go unpunished; for the maternal Tenderness of their Mothers either starved by their Necessities, or drowned in Gin; and, for a Trifle, conceal and forgive an Offence which our Laws have made Capital.'[10]

Fielding may have been too harsh on London mothers; to be sure, their lives were often characterized by squalid starvation, but not only mercenary motives kept them out of the courts. The London populace often settled their disputes among themselves, relying on shaming assailants among the neighbours, and forcing them to apologize and pay a small amount as compensation rather than attempting to make their way through the expensive, complicated legal system. Women took justice into their own hands to punish child molesters: In 1793, a 'respectable' man accused of raping two charity children was 'by a vast crowd of women (one of whom cut the tail off his hair) hissed, hooted, and hunted to his dwelling house' after the magistrate dismissed the case.[11] Women may have been more enraged about the sexual abuse of children than men. When Mrs Poultney, the wife of a powder-flask maker, found that a coachman had assaulted her four-year-old daughter, she told her husband, 'What does the fellow mean by playing tricks with my child. I'll go and kick up a dust with him; he said pho, pho, the coachman is always playing with the children.'[12]

Adult women who had been sexually assaulted, however, could not necessarily rely on neighbourhood sanctions to punish their assailants, for as we have seen, popular culture contained strong misogynist elements. Although there are many accounts of popular justice inflicted on offenders in cases of abandonment, infidelity, spouse abuse, or sodomy, rape cases rarely incited charivari or rough music. The exception is from the North Riding of Yorkshire, where if a man had 'abused a girl' he was often 'tripped up, seized, and mounted on a stand or pole, and serenaded' by groups of women. If he refused to marry a girl he had impregnated, he was forced to flee the countryside. However, it is not clear what 'abused' meant, whether it was sexual assault or another violation of the codes of courtship.[13] This is not surprising, for charivaris were often an outgrowth of masculine popular culture, and until the early nineteenth century revealed their hostility to women by punishing wives who dominated their husbands. In fact, rough music could be inflicted against rape victims who dared prosecute. In 1817, after a Bedfordshire man was executed for rape, 200 persons surrounded the victim's house, 'exhibiting obscene effigies of herself and her parents'.[14] A century earlier, when John Vizard was charged with rape and defamation, he organized 'a parade of armed men with rough music', and 'terrified the constable of the town'.[15] The actions of the young men in these instances reflected the belief that rape shamed the victim, not the assailant.

Deprived, therefore, of the sanctions of popular justice, many women were doubtless too intimidated, ashamed or friendless even to accuse their attackers before a magistrate. As one female correspondent to the *Universal Register* commented in response to yet another acquittal of an alleged rapist, 'I almost think some of the poor sufferers, who are unwilling to expose their misfortune in a court of justice, are now lamenting their injury in silent sadness, rather than submitting to public shame.'[16] As is still too often the case today, a trial for rape ended up putting the victim on trial, an experience most assaulted women probably wished to avoid.

Most rapes of adult women were never even prosecuted, for from the moment she escaped her assailant a woman had to fight for her rights against a corrupt legal system constructed to benefit those who were rich and male. If a woman was angry enough to bring charges, her friends and relatives often encouraged her to settle the matter out of court. In fact, magistrates often instructed victims of any common assault to 'make it up', i.e. to pardon the assailant once he or she apologized and paid a small sum though rape was a much more serious crime than common assault.[17] For some women, however, compensation of a few pence was not enough: they felt angry at being assaulted, rather than ashamed at their loss of chastity. Mrs Sarah Bethell, for example, presumably did expose Robert Moody to all their neighbours, but she also fought her way through the courts all the way to the Old Bailey.

The first obstacle Mrs Bethell faced was the corruption of the legal system. She had to pay a constable or watchman a shilling for a warrant, which could have amounted to several days' wages, and even then, the official would concentrate on harassing 'disorderly women' from the streets rather than arresting her assailant. Thomas Taylor, a Southwark constable, gave Robert Moody 'all the lenity in the world' and allowed four days to lapse between the issuance of the warrant and his arrest.[18]

Once accused, many assailants attempted to bribe their victims to drop the charges; given the extreme poverty of the average eighteenth-century labouring women, guineas may have overcome desire for revenge. For instance, Jonathan Thompson, a gentleman, successfully avoided trial by paying servant Anne Greenwall for clothes, expenses, and coach fare to London from Newcastle to get her out of the way.[19] Thomas Scott and James Sherlock sent a message from a Cumberland gaol to the woman they had raped and robbed, offering her five guineas if she would drop the charges; although she refused, they were found not guilty.[20] While such bribes obviously flowed from the pervasive monetary lubrication of the legal system, they also stemmed from a more specific valuation of female sexual property. For instance, landlord Edward Hatfield paid the common-law husband of Ann Clarke three guineas in an unsuccessful effort to prevent her from prosecuting him for a particularly brutal rape.[21] He seemed to believe compensation was owed to her husband, not her, for the rape.

Hatfield did not succeed in deterring Mrs Clarke from prosecuting, but his corrupt attempts did not stop there.

Threatening to bribe witnesses, he told her common-law husband that 'he would lay ten guineas I was a common prostitute, and that four of his men had to do with me.'[22] Perjury was extremely common in eighteenth-century courts, though it is impossible to know exactly how many witnesses were bribed without discovery.

The corruption of the legal system extended beyond bent witnesses and mercenary constables to magistrates and judges themselves. London magistrates during the late eighteenth century were notorious for taking bribes from prostitutes or even being involved in brothels. In fact in 1786 the *Universal Register* reported that a magistrate, 'remarkable for his avidity in sending the perambulating fair' to Bridewell, was about to be charged at the Old Bailey Sessions for rape. Unsurprisingly, the case never came to trial.[23] In 1778 John Gretton, a Middlesex Justice, 'arrested a woman without warrant and confined her to his house for eight hours', where he 'rummaged and pulled her about', releasing her only on payment of considerable fee.[24]

Yet it was not only corruption, but misogynist, patriarchal principles which blocked women's attempts to gain redress for rape through the legal system. Even the most honest eighteenth-century jurist regarded rape victims' claims unsympathetically. The novelist Henry Fielding, who served as an influential magistrate at Bow Street in Covent Garden, viewed rape victims' claims with harsh scepticism even before he assumed office. In his 1731 play, 'Rape upon Rape', Fielding portrayed rape charges as attempts to blackmail respectable men. He did not believe 'unchaste' women had any right to prosecute for rape: as one victim is told by a constable in the play, 'If you are not a woman of virtue, why you will be whipped for accusing a gentleman of robbing you of what you had not to lose.'[25] As a magistrate Fielding continued to regard rape victims unsympathetically. In his *Covent Garden Journal*, which he published to alert the public to crime, highway robberies featured much more prominently than rape. Of eight cases of rape noted in the years 1752 to 1754, he reported four in the most sceptical manner, claiming they were false accusations. Fielding allowed bail to one 'housekeeper of reputation' charged with rape, though by law the man should have been imprisoned to await trial; he noted that this was a common practice of magistrates, 'For was it otherwise, no man living could say this night, that he was certain he should not lie in Newgate tomorrow.'[26]

London magistrates later in the century continued to disbelieve rape victims. In 1786, the *Morning Chronicle* characterized country Justices as gullible provincials lacking 'immediate access to the best legal advice; they are very often much difficulted when women of loose character or equivocal virtue come before them and swear a rape.'[27]

The case of Mary Beek, a servant, illuminates how magistrates refused to take many cases seriously. She testified that her assailant, an acquaintance, had tried to kiss her despite her resistance, dragged her into the bedroom, and attempted to rape her. The magistrates, however, noted that 'the girl had permitted him to take liberties with her and not having made complaint earlier . . . . The Magistrates were of the opinion that she consented to what passed.'[28] Her plight was typical, for most rape accusations, in fact, never went beyond the magistrates' court. The Guildhall Justice Room minute books of 1780 to 1796 reveal that out of seventeen men charged with rape or assault with intent to rape of females over twelve, only one man was tried in the Old Bailey Sessions, and he was found not guilty. In three other cases assailants were formally charged but never prosecuted. In four cases, magistrates dismissed the charges, and in nine cases the rapist was never apprehended. In the North-east circuit the proportion of prosecuted rapes was higher, but still low. Out of forty-five depositions from adult women in the years 1779 to 1799, 36 per cent or sixteen were apparently dismissed by magistrates, or the assailant never apprehended.

Mrs Bethell did not only have to convince the magistrate of her case; a grand jury assessed the validity of accusations, reserving great scepticism for rape cases. In the North-east circuit, grand juries threw out at least 20 per cent of such charges by marking them 'no true bill',[29] although generally grand juries passed one in seven indictments. Once a rape victim's charge had passed all these hurdles, she still had to

make the long and expensive journey to the city where assizes
were held. Bribes and threats often successfully deterred
victims from testifying in court; 11 per cent of the rape trials
in the North-east circuit were aborted when the prosecutrix
or witnesses failed to appear. As a result of these compounded
difficulties, in the North-east circuit only one third of men
accused of rape of adult women were ever tried.

Then as now, trials for rape were more of an ordeal for the
victim than the accused man. The pomp and ceremony of the
Assizes and the Old Bailey Courts must have intimidated
many women and their witnesses. The Assizes were the main
social event in provincial towns, and attended by well-dressed
audiences. Before the court came into session, the bewigged
and robed judges and the local notables would proceed
through the town. In London, the Old Bailey Court was held
throughout the year, and it was feared as the place where
many of the labouring poor were sent to their deaths or
transported for petty crimes. It was an extremely public
court: not only were the transcripts printed and sold as
pamphlets, but the London populace packed into the court
and cheered or booed the accused, the prosecutrix and
witnesses.[30]

The ordeal began when the Judge asked the victim to
describe in detail how the rape occurred. Male judges,
counsels, juries and spectators were obsessed with the explicit
sexual details of rape. Judges and counsels would subject a
victim to rigorous cross-examination, questioning her as to
how her assailant could stop her mouth, hold down her
hands, pull up her petticoats and pull down his breeches all at
the same time. In part, this curiosity stemmed from crude
prurience; rape victims sometimes faced laughter from the
galleries when they attempted to testify and transcripts of
rape trials were sold as titillating literature. Although the
Universal Register complained that the 'liberties which the
flippant pleaders are allowed to give themselves in the cross-
examination' of rape victims increased the incidence of rape,
this newspaper more often dismissed any accusation of sexual
abuse as 'without the smallest foundation'.[31] Barristers and
doctors, no doubt reflecting widespread popular belief,

asserted that a healthy adult woman could not be raped.[32] These insinuations were even applied when many of these victims were young girls raped by their masters, who had the power of the employer as well as the power of adult male strength over their adolescent servants.

The curiosity about minute details of rape also derived from a patriarchal concern with chastity: what mattered was whether penile penetration and ejaculation had occurred and the hymen broken, thus damaging the victim's value as sexual property. By the 1780s, some judges began to insist on evidence of ejaculation in order to condemn men to death, evidence which women found it extremely difficult to provide.[33]

Women's testimony dramatically differed from the legal discourses of judges. Women expressed their feelings of outrage and stressed their injuries rather than the sexual details of assaults. Rape victims preferred to use euphemisms to describe what happened to them, and expressed embarrassment at having to testify explicitly. Eleanor Mathews, a servant, replied to the judge's request to be more specific by exclaiming, 'I asked your pardon, I hope you will excuse me for mentioning these things; I have spoken it very plainly . . . he laid with me, and I was very ill afterwards.' Finally, after repeated urgings, she said, 'he put his private parts to my private parts'.[34]

Such hesitation stemmed from modesty and a sense of privacy rather than a woman's inability to articulate what happened to her, or lack of sexual knowledge. Child victims of rape in this period were quite anatomically explicit in their testimony; almost invariably they said, 'he put his cock (or private parts) into my private parts – it hurt very much.' Adult victims, unlike children, had learned colloquial euphemisms for sexual behaviour, but they knew exactly what they meant. Sexually experienced women such as Mary Hunt, who had lived with several men, preferred to use less explicit terminology than judges required. When pressed in court to describe what happened to her, she testified, 'he forced me very much to go with him, and what he had he had out; he tried very hard to go with me.' Finally she said, 'he tried to carnally know me.'[35]

Mary Hunt's modesty did not result from shame or timidity. After she described how she had been raped, the judge commented, 'What injury you might receive in those parts would not hurt you know, you had tried that before', adding with heavy sarcasm, 'the moment you saw his breeches down, it must alarm a lady of your delicate sensibilities . . .' It took great courage and anger for a woman such as Mary Hunt to face such public humiliation in the courtroom. Although she obviously felt she had a right to prosecute, the judge refused to believe her testimony since she was not a virgin and was not badly injured. When he scornfully queried her on the absence of bruises, she finally burst out, 'Then you think a woman is not hurt, unless she is quite killed.'[36]

For the judge, however, the fact that Mary Hunt cohabited with a guardsman ruined her character, and therefore her credibility; her injuries were irrelevant. Despite the lawbook's assertion that even a harlot had the right to prosecute for a rape, judges always allowed testimony impugning a woman's reputation. The Courts judged the behaviour of women by restrictive upper-class standards of feminine behaviour which presented an extreme contrast to the mores of plebeian London. Unlike the genteel heroines of sentimental novels, who considered speaking to a man as forward, London working women ranging from respectable shopkeepers to rough porters drank at pubs with male acquaintances and only intermittently concerned themselves with the bonds of legal marriage. For judges and juries, any hint of such behaviour often led to instant verdicts of not guilty despite conclusive evidence of rape; they considered that such women did not have chastity worth damaging. For instance, Ralph Cutler escaped punishment for raping Mrs Mary Bradley, the wife of an auctioneer, because she had been seen playing skittles with him at Merlin's Caves.[37] Robert Moody was acquitted of raping his acquaintance Mrs Sarah Bethell after a neighbour insinuated she was vulgar.[38]

Men often did not bother to claim that the victim had consented or deny they committed a rape; if she had a bad reputation, rape simply was not regarded as a crime. In half the trials in the Old Bailey for this period (for rapes of females over twelve) impugning a woman's character sufficed to gain accused men a verdict of not guilty. Twenty-two per cent also escaped on minor technical points, for judges directed juries to acquit on the grounds of irrelevant inconsistencies in the victim's testimony, such as whether her sister cooked meat or fish for supper or if she told two or three housemaids about the assault.[39] Evidence that the victim's relatives and the assailant discussed 'making it up' also lead to acquittals even if the victim refused to discuss such bribes.

The focus on the victim's character contrasted with the usual practice in eighteenth-century courts, in which the severity of punishment depended heavily on the accused's character. For instance, if a man stole some bread because his family was starving, but his neighbours asserted his usual honesty, a judge would let him off lightly; if he was a notorious thief, he might be hung. However, a man's sexual reputation seemed to be irrelevant. Although three people had witnesed Frederick Thomas and Christopher Ayres raping Isabella Ray in an alley, and had overheard them brag about the assault, they were acquitted of raping and murdering her, perhaps because their employer testified to their characters.[40] Jeremiah Amenet was similarly given a good character and acquitted of the rape of his apprentice, thirteen-year-old Mary Martin, although she had immediately told neighbour women about the assault and a midwife testified she had been ill-used.[41] If a man had been charged with other assaults besides rape, he could still escape punishment.

Even if it was clear that a woman had been sexually assaulted without her consent, judges could refuse to define the assault as rape. A judge recommended a not guilty verdict for William Hodge, accused of raping his sixteen-year-old servant, declaring,

It is a very brutal thing, for which this fellow deserves to be punished in a way more severe than he has been, or will be; to be sure, taking any method to persuade a girl, his

> servant, of this age, in his house, under his protection, he
> having a wife and three children, one cannot assume
> anything more brutal and beastly than his conduct; but as
> to a rape, there is no pretence.[42]

Hodge had broken down her locked garret door, and threatened to 'knock her brains out' if she resisted. She said the assault hurt her and she continued to be very ill.

In practice, British judges and juries refused to take rape victims seriously; they almost never regarded the rape of an adult woman as a punishable offense. In the London Old Bailey Court between 1770 and 1800, out of forty-three men tried for rapes of females over twelve, only three were found guilty (and two of them had raped fourteen-year-old girls). In the North-east assize circuit for the same period, only two of fifteen men tried for rape of adult women were condemned.

The low conviction rate cannot be dismissed as a mere symptom of the corruption and inefficiency of eighteenth-century justice. As Nazife Bashar notes, juries found it easy to convict even teenagers to death for minor thefts, but they hesitated to condemn members of their own sex for brutal rapes of women.[43]

Eighteenth-century justice, therefore, made no pretence of protecting a woman from sexual assault unless she could claim the status of the sexual property of a patriarch. Standing before the bar, a male and female thief were equally oppressed under the law; but the male rapist, no matter what his class, had the full weight of patriarchal justice on his side. The awful sentence of death proclaimed upon a pickpocket was intended to impress the unruly populace with the sanctity of property; but the ease with which rapists escaped punishment, and the humiliation their victims faced in court, must have effectively told men that the law cared little for the integrity of women's bodies. However outspoken, vigorous and angry eighteenth-century women could be, their protests remained unheard. In the early nineteenth century, women's ability to protest rape diminished still further; as the next chapter shows, the shift from apathy to chivalrous protection in legal practice on rape only served to allow experts, not women, to define sexual violence.

CHAPTER 4

Silent suffering: law and medicine in the early nineteenth century

The protection of female chastity greatly concerned early nineteenth-century moralists, who extolled the attention paid to female honour as proof of England's high civilization. Several reforms enacted during this period eased prosecution for rape in British courts; however, they were accompanied by an increasing regulation of female sexual behaviour, and the suppression of women's ability to protest about rape.

Working women were now judged by the increasingly rigid standards of separate spheres and Evangelical morality. The ideal lady was passionless; while this may have enabled middle-class women to claim moral superiority over men,[1] it discredited less conventional females far more. At worst, 'fallen' women were scorned as predatory creatures who lured young men to sin; at best, they could be pitied as victims of male lust. This pity, however, had a price; it required the seduced maiden to acknowledge the taint of her own sin, and passively accept her plight. The rape victim who tried to gain redress violated this decorum with her anger, for she also broke the taboo on female speech about sex.

In fact, a proliferation of medical, legal and religious writings defined the woman who defied this proscription as deviant herself.[2] The Foucauldian 'discursive explosion' about sex, which issued from the pens of male moralists, doctors and lawyers, silenced women's ability to protest about rape.[3] These experts wished to reserve to themselves the power to speak about sex. Their obsessive morality obscured the true facts of rape; they claimed a chaste woman should be

59

so modest she could not speak or even know about sexual violence. Their continual flood of discourses – ostensibly based on religious, legal, or medical expertise – were in essence concerned with the patriarchal control of female sexuality. Legislation about prostitution, unmarried mothers, and rape all aimed to force women to conform to the control of men in the institution of marriage. A woman's submission to the control of husband or father always defined her chastity; rape violated not her bodily integrity but the patriarchal ownership of her sexuality.

The increased efficiency and diminished corruption of the British legal system did bring more rapists to justice during this period. In the North-east assize circuit, for instance, 54 per cent of accusations of rape on females over twelve resulted in trials between 1800 and 1829, as opposed to 33 per cent between 1770 and 1799. Legal reformers began to view the extremely low conviction rate as a problem which should be remedied. In 1828, Sir Robert Peel successfully introduced legislation which removed the more onerous technical requirements for proving violation: victims no longer had to testify to emission, and any degree of penetration became defined as rape, especially in cases of the rape of children. Previously, evidence that the hymen was broken (in the case of virgins) had been required.[4] In the 1830s cases of indecent assault began to be tried in the Old Bailey Sessions and punished with sentences ranging from two months to three years, although it is possible these were actually attempted rapes or rapes tried on lesser charges to increase the likelihood of conviction. The death penalty for rape was thought to prevent juries from reaching guilty verdicts; when it was finally amended to transportation for life in 1841, the conviction rate increased from 10 per cent between 1836 and 1840 to 33 per cent between 1841 and 1845.[5]

Expertise and emission: doctors versus victims

By examining more closely the 1828 legislation abolishing the requirement of proving emission, we can begin to see how these apparent reforms actually suppressed women's ability to speak out against rape. Doctors and lawyers wished to establish definitions of rape based on 'scientific' criteria such as ejaculation, but their expertise foundered on the blunt necessity of patriarchal control. Ultimately, the technical value of this tangible evidence of rape evaporated when faced with the prospect of allowing women to testify about such sexual details.

The 1828 legislation actually reversed a precedent only established in the late eighteenth century, when some judges began to pronounce that the victim must testify that her assailant had ejaculated. Despite the fact that eminent writers such as Hale and East did not require such evidence, many justices after 1781 followed this strict rule.[6]

There were four reasons for this opinion. First, proof of ejaculation seemed to satisfy legal and medical experts as a tangible sign of rape which they could codify; they could observe the physical evidence of semen rather than relying on the victim's testimony. Medical jurisprudence, claiming a scientific ability to prove the facts of assaults, was established as a discipline during this period.[7] Second, judges may have required such rigid proof of rape in order to avoid executing rapists for the capital felony; instead, they could be acquitted and possibly charged with attempted rape. Third, establishing proof of emission gave magistrates, judges and doctors an excuse to ask victims humiliatingly explicit questions. By the second decade of the nineteenth century, assize depositions from the North-east assize circuit reveal that magistrates apparently asked women not only if the assailant had ejaculated but also how far he penetrated, how he moved, and the duration of the act.

An intensified concern with women's chastity as property lies at the heart of this matter. If a rapist had emitted sperm into his victim, she could become pregnant, producing an illegitimate child. On a more emotional level, men seemed to view ejaculation as a physical pollution or despoilation of a woman, rendering her damaged property forever. The medical writer Chitty made this clear when he expressed his doubts about the 1828 law:

> . . . there is a natural delicate, though perhaps
> indescribable feeling that deters most men who know that a
> female has been completely violated, though manifestly
> after every effort of resistance, from taking her in marriage,
> but does not exist, at least in so powerful a degree, if he be
> certain the sexual intercourse was incomplete according to
> the ancient law of rape.[8]

Despite these qualms, the fact that the emission requirement made it almost impossible to convict a man for rape was
the ostensible reason for its abolition. Aside from the fact that
many rapists do not ejaculate, a woman's terror and pain, not
to speak of ignorance, often prevented her from perceiving
this occurrence. Of course, any sort of penetration or attempt
to penetrate can be equally traumatic for the victim. The
popular belief that female consent and orgasm were necessary
for conception, ratified as late as 1815 by Dr Samuel Farr,
exacerbated the difficulties of women attempting to prove this
crime.[9]

But at heart, moralists objected to the notion that proof of
ejaculation actually allowed any 'profligate' woman to convict
a man for rape. Lawyers, doctors and moralists wished to
invest the power of proving rape in their own moral
judgments, not in women's words or bodies.

Experts on medical jurisprudence found that this task
required an assertion of their own authority over the
interpretation of hard medical facts. In textbook after
textbook, authorities declared that the absence of the hymen,
and the presence of bruises, inflammation, new infections of
venereal disease, and semen residues, could not be taken as
proof of rape in conjunction with a woman's testimony,[10] for
if doctors relied on such forensic evidence, it would prove
that 'unchaste' women could be sexually assaulted. And
'unchaste' did not merely mean women with considerable
sexual experience, such as prostitutes, for a virgin could be
considered 'immodest'. As Dr Michael Ryan noted, physical
evidence itself could not prove a rape. He advised police
surgeons that:

> The presence of the reputed signs of virginity afford no

decisive proof of chastity, nor their absence no decisive proof of incontinence. If all the reputed signs described above exist, the female feels offended at the examination, or rather displays evidence of shame; if her morals, age, and education have been good, then there are strong grounds for supposing her in possession of chastity; and if all the contrary signs exist with a suspected reputation, and an equivocal virtue, then there is reason to pronounce a contrary opinion . . .[11]

In fact, moral objections to women recounting explicit details in open court seem to have provided the main impetus behind the 1828 legislation. As the *Morning Chronicle* editorialized, 'No modest woman can possibly comprehend what is meant by these questions.'[12] If the victim of rape could testify that emission had occurred, her frankness branded her as immodest, and her assailant as less culpable. The *Morning Chronicle* even declared that:

. . . no female not uninitiated into vice, or neglected in education, can possibly go through the ordeal of a public trial; and the father is not to be envied who would not rather allow the injury to his daughter to escape punishment, than hear the daughter answer those questions, which . . . must be put to her, before a conviction can be obtained.[13]

The suppression of women's speech

The stress on modest language paralyzed rape victims, for any woman who prosecuted for rape had to speak publicly about sex and expose her loss of chastity, behaviour inconsistent with maidenly purity. More and more, women hesitated to report sexual assaults, fearing rape would be seen as a taint upon their reputations. As Lambeth magistrate Mr Coombe noted, 'the more decent or respectable females were, the more reluctant they were in coming forward to give public details of such gross outrages.'[14] Dressmaker Theresa Reynolds testified that she had told a fellow lodger, 'If it were not for the shame of having my name in the newspaper, I would make him repent his conduct,' several days before she charged him with an indecent assault.[15]

Unlike their eighteenth-century counterparts, rape victims in the North-east began to express feelings of shame and hesitation at reporting assaults to the authorities after 1807. Mary Chapman, the daughter of a pitman, waited for six weeks before telling her mother she had been raped: 'her mother then struck her and said O Mary for shame.'[16] Elizabeth Leeming stated 'the reason why she did not make a complaint to a justice sooner, was that she was afraid to tell it publicly, and that she would not have come if her mother had not made her come; that she shamed with it (sic).'[17] Young victims were especially reluctant to tell even their mothers about assaults. Anne Cooper, thirteen, waited three or four days to tell her mother, despite the fact that she 'cried when she went to bed, because I was frightened by the prisoner'; she feared her mother would beat her. The judge also considered the assault to be shameful, but in a different way: he directed the jury to acquit the prisoner on the grounds that 'it would be better for the public morals' if the case did not go further.[18]

Sexual ignorance, while not as widespread as it was later to become, increasingly handicapped women's efforts to articulate what happened to them. In the eighteenth century, women who testified in trials spoke in euphemisms such as 'he had his way with me', but they did so out of modesty and a sense of privacy; ultimately, they seemed to know exactly what they meant. In the early nineteenth century, women began to use even vaguer terminology which invariably obscured the seriousness of sexual assault. They were unable to make clear to others exactly what had happened to them. For instance, Ann Chandler, the seventeen-year-old daughter of a boatbuilder, told one neighbour 'she had been ill-used by some man, who had taken liberties with her'; to another, she cried, the man had 'insulted' her; but neither understood that 'force had been used against her'. As a result, magistrates dismissed her charge of rape against Edward Hooper.[19]

Sometimes women simply did not know what rape meant,

and their ignorance enabled men to escape punishment. In 1834, Eliza Randall was hurt enough after her tailor fiancé assaulted her to require a medical examination, but she did not realize she had been raped until the doctor told her so. The magistrate refused to commit her assailant for rape, because she had not been aware of the nature of the assault at the time it happened.[20] Phoebe Lawson was found drowned in a pond several days after she had charged Charles Lowther Jones with having 'connection with her against her will'. Finding him not guilty of rape, the Judge said, 'from what had been stated to him by the surgeon, the poor girl did not know what was meant by the word "rape" which was used in the deposition.'[21]

Despite this focus on modesty and the overwhelming nature of legal and expert discourses, many women continued to regard rape as something that should taint the assailant, not his victim. Harriet Rainford, a York matchgirl, told a watchman that Thomas Galand had 'ill-used her and ought to be ashamed of himself'.[22] Mary Ann Rawson's mother declared 'It was a scandalous shame' that her daughter had been raped by her master.[23] Like their eighteenth-century counterparts, they believed the law's promise to punish assaults committed on them. As Elizabeth Pullen told John Burroughs, 'He should have the worst the law could do for him,' – and he was one of the few who did.[24]

The punishment of the victim

Given the increased legal surveillance over the sexual behaviour of working-class women, women who infringed the bounds of modesty by accusing a man of rape could be punished themselves. Police and magistrates, accustomed to treating prostitutes and vagrant women harshly, rarely became more sympathetic to victims of rape. In fact, a woman could be arrested for indecent exposure while being assaulted. A middle-aged 'lady of independent fortune' named Mrs Elizabeth Brierly was committed to the sessions along with a Pimlico baker with whom she had been found, despite her protest that 'he had seized me round the waist, and behaved indecently, and I was very much pulled around and bruised.'[25] Mrs Winter, 'the wife of a respectable individual residing at Brentford', was similarly charged even though she claimed at the time she had been 'ill-used' and her clothes were torn. While she escaped imprisonment, she had to post sureties to appear at sessions.[26]

Attempting to escape punishment for indecent assault, men who molested women on the street sometimes accused their victims of theft. A 'gentleman of the law' accused 'a well-dressed female' of having stolen his watch after they shared a cab, but the cabdriver testified he 'had taken great liberties with the lady'. She was discharged, after admitting 'she certainly had been silly enough to take a share of the cab.'[27] Fanny Hoggett, a 'young married woman of respectable appearance', was discharged after Mr Henry Edmonds, a grazier and cattle-dealer, accused her of stealing his gold pin. It transpired that he accosted and propositioned her on Mile End Road, and 'used her roughly' when she indignantly refused.[28]

The imprisonment of women who wished to prosecute for rape most starkly illustrates the nineteenth-century obsession with the protection of public morality rather than the protection of women. Every person who prosecuted had to provide sureties to guarantee that she would appear at the assizes or sessions: poor women without husbands or fathers could not do so, and thus became liable to imprisonment themselves when more wealthy assailants could go free on bail. Magistrates allowed prosecutions for rape when the crime offended public decency, but seemed to regard its victims as equally offensive. In an 1800 *cause célèbre*, Mary Rich, a fourteen-year-old workingman's daughter who accused a lawyer of raping her, was imprisoned for a month in solitary confinement and fed on bread and water, while the lawyer went free on bail.[29] In Leicester, Mrs Naomi MacDonald was imprisoned after charging two boatmen with rape, being unable to provide sureties. Not surprisingly, 'upon being brought to court . . . she cried and raved and went into hysterics . . . it was understood that only her feelings, not her reason, were affected.'[30]

Her discourses as deviant

Once a woman succeeded in bringing her prosecution to court, she faced judges intent on scrutinizing her own discourse for signs of immodesty. A jury dismissed charges against George Spicer immediately after his victim, Elizabeth Senthouse, testified, for as the *Leeds Intelligencer* noted, 'Her evidence was of such a nature, and given with such flippancy, that the jury, without any further witnesses, declared themselves satisfied that little violence had been used.'[31] If women used colloquial terms, the only terms they knew, to describe what happened to them, upper-class judges would brand them as immoral. Reporting the trial of a man for raping a nineteen-year-old barmaid in Sunderland, *The Times* noted that when she described the rape 'she stated the gross expression frequent in the mouth of sailors which he applied to her,' and went on to say that the surgeon who examined her 'used a technical description instead of her terms respecting the manner in which the offense was committed, and this appeared to be a contradiction to her present testimony, but she stated the deposition had been explained to her as meaning what she had now sworn.' The judge induced the jury to find the man not guilty, stating, 'It would have been better if she had declined to repeat the coarse sailor terms,' and disapprovingly noted her 'presence of mind during the violence of her struggle'.[32]

Presence of mind, then, was taken as an indication of immodesty, but if a woman followed the rules of feminine behaviour too well she could not provide evidence with which to convict a man. Mrs Jane Rockett testified before a magistrate that she had been raped by the son of the farmer who employed her, but faced with the pomp of the assize court, she remained silent when asked to give the particulars of the event, and he was immediately acquitted.[33]

The spectre of the vengeful woman falsely accusing an innocent man of rape haunted legal reformers. In 1828 and 1829, the *Morning Chronicle* continually cited supposed incidents of unjust accusations of rape to illustrate the inefficiency of juries and the subjection of poor men to the vagaries of British justice.[34] The *Morning Chronicle*'s concern derived less from serious legal principles than from a pervasive male refusal to believe women's words; it mirrored a plebeian image of the deceitful woman.

Songs about false swearing may have encouraged juries to disbelieve women's testimony. A ballad entitled 'The Wicked Woman of Chigwell' derides a Mrs Harrison, who claimed that a Dr Saunders assaulted her in bed; implying she had been a prostitute, it declared, 'She ought to be well-bonnetted, and put in the prison van.'[35] Thomas Hegan was the hero of 'Fanny Blair', a popular song about his conviction for rape and execution on the testimony of an eleven-year-old girl of that name. He warns,

> Beware of false swearing and all sad perjury,
> For by a young female I'm wounded full soon,
> You see I am cut down in the height of my bloom.[36]

Even the testimony of child victims of sexual assault could be portrayed as malicious by newspaper accounts. Twelve-year-old Maria Bailey, assaulted by an old soldier, was described as 'a rather pretty looking girl, but with an expression of artfulness and cunning about her eyes'. The man was acquitted.[37] Another reporter noted of Anne Murphy, also twelve, that 'the little girl told a very disgusting story, with unusual flippancy' although her assailant was convicted to six months hard labour.[38] Surgeons corroborated this notion of the wicked working-class child, sexually depraved at an early age.[39] Dr Ryan declared that 'depraved mothers have induced their children to make accusations against innocent persons,' and that gonorrhea in children could result from non-venereal disease.[40] His claims were influential in practice, for he testified in at least one rape case invalidating the testimony of a young girl.[41] Another surgeon, a Mr Leeson, proclaimed that it was 'physically impossible' to rape a child and his testimony resulted in the acquittal of at least one man accused of this crime.[42] By 1844 Alfred S. Taylor found it necessary in his medical jurisprudence textbook to remind doctors that 'it must not be assumed by medical witnesses that all these charges of rape on young children are frivolous, and that they impute an impossible crime.'[43]

Rape victims whose prosecutions failed could actually be tried for perjury. After he was acquitted of drugging and violating Emma Munton, a servant, a chemist named Mr Morse charged her with accusing him falsely. With the help of his servants' alibis, Morse proved to the judge's satisfaction that he could not have been her assailant; nonetheless, the judge discharged Emma because he believed she had merely identified the wrong man.[44] In 1819, Samuel Mills, 'a man of gentlemanly appearance', charged his former servant Hannah Whitehorn with perjury after she unsuccessfully accused him of rape.[45] In a similar case, William Smith charged Elizabeth Roebuck, his former servant, with perjury after she testified he had raped another servant. It is not surprising that his accusation met with scepticism, for he had previously been charged with indecent assault on an eight-year-old girl and also with trying to hang a woman.[46] Even though prosecutions for perjury often failed, the imprisonment and humiliation suffered by these women could effectively deter many victims from prosecuting rapists.

The discourse of the rape victim, then, was defined as immoral and deceitful: not only did she violate the principles of feminine modesty, but she usurped the privilege of masculine experts to define sexual crime. Experts' definitions of sexual crime, however, did not derive from the internal logic of law or medicine. They merely cloaked popular patriarchal assumptions with the mantle of scientific authority.

The case of consent

The legal and medical definition of consent is a case in point. In the early nineteenth century, an increased concern with the protection of chastity required assailants to justify their actions more than they had in the previous era. As a result, these men often claimed a woman 'consented' to whatever violence they used. This consent was never defined as a product of a woman's own will; it derived from her status as chaste or unchaste. While legal authority Edward Hyde East declared, 'It is no mitigation of this offense (rape) that the woman at last yielded to the violence, if such her consent was forced by death or duress,'[47] many judges accepted defendants' claims that women consented to violence.

The notion that women 'consented to violence' does not often appear in eighteenth-century trials. Its appearance in the early nineteenth century may have been symptomatic of the increasingly pervasive view that women did not particularly enjoy sex and submitted to it only from fear, duty, or love. While this view was certainly not universal, it conveniently dovetailed with the notion that violence was normal in sexual intercourse, a notion prevalent in a sexual economy in which chastity became a valuable property women were reluctant to surrender.[48]

Assailants, doctors and judges alike shared these views. Repeatedly, defendants saw no contradiction between admitting they had raped a woman and asserting that she consented. A London publican, for instance, defended himself by claiming not only that another man had committed the rape on his barmaid, but that 'she had been a consenting party.'[49] An engineer charged with attempted rape on a fourteen-year-old pauper girl pleaded that he had been intoxicated and 'had no recollection of having used any violence or persuasion toward the girl.'[50] In one dramatic case from 1836, Henry Roper confessed to having raped a farmer's daughter and leaving her to die of cold thirty years before. A serious illness led to his conversion and confession of his past crime, but he would only state that he 'took her for a travelling woman, and he ravished her – that was, he had concerns with her, but he did not lay violent hands on her.' Mr Justice Park encouraged the jury to ignore his confession, observing, 'The prisoner, by the explanation he had given of what he meant by the word ravished, had shown that he gave to it a certain popular meaning, different from its significance in a legal and technical sense.'[51]

However popular this significance may have been, judges, magistrates and doctors gave it their authority by themselves equating violence and intercourse with consent. For instance, Elizabeth Dixon, servant in a Bishopsgate lodging house, went to the police court at Mansion House to charge a lodger ('of very respectable appearance') with raping her. But there a surgeon testified, 'There is not the least proof of recent violence.' The Lord Mayor asked, 'The violence had taken place long before?' and the surgeon replied, 'No doubt of it. I told her so, and she admitted she had been intimate with a gentleman two years before.'[52] In the trial of William Hall for the murder of Betty Minshull, a Warrington publican found strangled in a privy, the judge asked the jury to consider, 'if though violence was used, it was with her consent.'[53]

Medical jurisprudence legitimized men's claims that women 'consented' to violence, repeating the common belief that no man could rape a healthy adult woman by himself. T.R. Beck wrote that 'contusions on various parts of the extremity and body . . . are compatible with final consent on the part of the female,' and others confirm this view.[54] Michael Ryan baldly stated, 'It is to be recollected that many women will not consent without some force.'[55]

The celebrated case of Mary Ashford, a Birmingham servant allegedly raped and murdered by Abraham Thornton, hinged on the evidence of medical jurisprudence. After his arrest, Thornton insisted that Mary Ashford had 'consented to connection' with him. The surgeon who examined the body corroborated Thornton, testifying, 'The lacerations might have been produced if the sexual intercourse had taken place by consent.'[56] Much evidence beyond Mary Ashford's dead body existed to show that Thornton had in fact brutally raped her and then threw her in a pond. In the field where her body was found, witnesses had seen footsteps, matching the shoes of Thornton and the victim, which seemed to show a man chasing a woman across a field. They saw the imprint of her body on the grass, marked by quantities of blood where her crotch had been, prints of a man's knees and toes beneath the prints of her legs, and on her body, heavy bruises on her arms in the shape of a man's hands.[57]

In fact, a woman's words, or the wounds she suffered, were irrelevant in the matter of her consent. Judges' statements in rape cases reveal that what determined a woman's consent was not whether or not she said yes or no to a particular act, but whether she had conducted herself as the sexual property of husband or father, or as common property of all men.[58] If a woman acted too freely – for instance, went drinking in pubs, or walking out with various men – her consent was assumed, or irrelevant.

Precedent did declare that it was no excuse for a rape that a woman was a 'common strumpet', following the principle of equal protection under the law. Yet East concluded that a woman's bad character could be admitted for the defence.[59] Several cases during the early nineteenth century confirmed East, beginning with Rex. *v.* Clarke in 1817 and Rex. *v.* Parker in 1829. Even when a victim was under twelve, evidence as to her 'general indecency' could be allowed, according to the 1834 case of Tissington. Justice Coleridge's remarks in Rex. *v.* Hallett, in which eight men had been accused of raping a prostitute, illuminate the implications of this precedent:

> It is well worthy of your consideration whether, although she at first objected, she might not afterwards (on finding that the prisoners were determined) have yielded to them, and in some degree consented; and this question is more deserving of your attention when you come to consider what sort of person she was, what sort of house she lodged in, and that she herself told them that she would make no objection if they came one at a time.[60]

Mr Justice Stephens epitomized this notion of a woman's consent in 1869, when he 'submitted that the true rule must be, that where the man is led from the conduct of the woman to believe he is not committing a crime known to the law, the act of connection cannot under any circumstances amount to a rape.'[61]

Juries and judges had obeyed this dictum long before Stephens articulated it. When the defence that the woman consented was used, it is clear that she did not have to indicate that she would consent to sexual intercourse at that time and place. Her status as unchaste was enough to make her consent irrelevant to any man at any time or place – even to gang rape on a freezing winter night. As Dumaresq writes, 'for the female victim of sexual offenses, the moment of consent is not determined by her, but by a series of statutes and legal practices that construct and control it.'[62]

The following cases illustrate the extent to which women's consent was disregarded. In Derby, two 'labouring lads sprang out from behind a hedge' and one 'assisted' the other in 'violating' Harriet Hartshorne, according to the newspaper account. The reporter admitted that the men assisted each other in the connection but questioned 'whether it was a rape at all' since the prosecutrix 'had by no means a good character' and her sister 'a very loose character indeed'.[63] A Norfolk jury refused to convict farmers Thomas Morley and Thomas Walker for raping Eliza Everet, a farm labourer, on the high road. Despite her evidence, a piece of cloth she had torn from Morley's coat, the jury disbelieved her since she supposedly swore to the magistrate that 'she had been criminally connected with young men since she was 14.'[64] Two men were acquitted of rape on Mary Major, a labourer's wife at Ealing, who had been drinking at the same pub as them. She said she did not consent to connection with two men, and there were signs of struggle where the incident occurred, but the jury believed the counsel for the defense who alleged she 'consented'.[65]

The most extreme case involved the rape of a weaver, Anne Keyston, by three men in front of a crowd of 100 people on Bisley Common, Gloucestershire. After hearing that she had spent the afternoon in a public house drinking with some of the men, the counsel for the prosecutrix stopped the case voluntarily, and the jury returned a verdict of not guilty. *The Times* commented,

> It was understood that this transaction, though clearly not warranting a conviction against the prisoners, was attended with circumstances indicating a state of manners and morals which we should scarcely have suspected to exist in any part of the country.[66]

No clearer statement could be made of the fact that rape

would rarely be punished if the victim transgressed the norms of feminine behaviour.

Conclusion

This chapter began with the paradox that legal reforms made it easier to convict rapists in the early nineteenth century, while the reformers themselves suppressed women's ability to protest against rape. Reformers viewed rape as a crime against public morality and decency, so they directed their most strenuous efforts at regulating women's sexual behaviour, especially that of working-class women. Their modifications to the laws on rape grew out of larger legislative programmes such as the New Police and the New Poor Law, which aimed at regulating public order and repressing the unruly working-class. They were formulated to protect the ideals of chastity rather than women themselves. The introduction of the New Police increasingly restricted women's freedom to traverse city and country; their powers to clear prostitutes from the street were intensified by the Vagrancy Acts of 1834 and 1844, which made any woman vulnerable to arrest for 'suspicious loitering'.[67] The bastardy clauses of the New Poor Law exonerated fathers of illegitimate children from any responsibility for their maintenance, placing the moral blame and financial burden on the shoulders of impoverished unmarried mothers. All in all, the legislative punishment of unchaste women outweighed the limited extent to which rapists faced greater danger of retribution.

By the early nineteenth century, experts defined rape as a moral problem which tainted its victim more than her assailant. As Foucault noted, Victorian morality was accomplished by an explosion of expert writings on sex: debates on emission, new textbooks on medical jurisprudence, legislative programmes on illegitimacy. When these 'experts' confronted the rape victim, they exerted power over her through their 'scientific' knowledge of law and medicine.

However, the repressive effect of discourses on rape cannot be reduced to a conflict between elite expertise and working-class women, as Foucauldians would have it. These legal and medical experts colluded with working-class rapists by suppressing women's right to define their own consent. Their expertise dissolved when they abandoned the rigours of forensic evidence or legal precedent to assert naked patriarchal principles. Doctors ignored the bruises and lacerations on women's bodies which attested to their violation; judges forgot the principles which held that even a harlot had the right to say no.

The dissemination of expert discourses drowned women's ability to speak out against rape themselves. The words of women who did protest remained hidden in dusty depositions; they were never heard in public. Around 1795, the Old Bailey stopped printing transcripts of rape and other sex crime trials on the grounds that they were too 'indecent' to expose to the eyes of the public. Although by the first decades of the nineteenth century newspapers began to report rape trials in depth, their accounts always heavily censored women's voices. While the angry words of eighteenth-century victims of rape had been largely ignored, in the nineteenth century women's discourses were scrutinized, transformed, and ultimately silenced by authorities and rapists alike. As the next chapter will show, most victims of rape never came to the courts, but they did not escape the humiliation of upper-class men judging their characters. If they applied to charitable institutions for relief, they had to present themselves as seduced maidens penitent for their sins.

CHAPTER 5

Seduced maidens: middle-class myths, working-class realities

Seduced women became the objects of great pity in the early nineteenth century. Endless scenes of virtuous maidens victimized by heartless libertines brought tears to the eyes of novel-readers and theatre-goers, who flocked to see *Black-eyed Susan* (1829) and *The Artizan's Daughter* (1845). The passive victim of a wicked seducer was also a favoured charitable object; she could be purified of her sin without contaminating her benefactor with prostitution's pollution.

Yet, as in the courts, the preservation of female chastity rather than the protection of women from violence inspired such concern. It did not matter if a fallen woman had been seduced by force or favours. Charitable discourses about the seduced woman, like legal discourses about the rape victim, centred more around determining her character for chastity than whether or not she had been the victim of violence.

The records of a London charitable institution which took in the infants of unmarried mothers reveal how this discourse of seduction distorted the reality of women's lives. Applicants were required to submit petitions detailing the circumstances of their pregnancies. Most of these unmarried mothers had not yielded to the allure of sin; rather, they had followed traditional courtship customs allowing premarital sex, while a significant minority said they had been raped. But the rhetoric of seduction blurred the distinction between these circumstances and made it difficult for many women to articulate the fact that force had been used against them.

These records do not only demonstrate how middle-class

discourses distorted working women's words; they also reveal a sexual crisis within the working class. The majority of women who had been raped named men who courted them as their assailants. The confusion between rape and seduction thus reflected men's behaviour as well as middle-class discourses.

The rhetoric of seduction

The officials of this institution belonged to one of the gentler traditions of early nineteenth-century charity. They regarded the objects of their benevolence not as immoral harlots but as 'poor victims of unprincipled seduction and brutal desertion'; they attacked the 'systematic profligacy' of seducers. Middle- and upper-class clergymen, magistrates, judges, and lawyers, their Evangelicalism led them to philanthropy rather than a more harsh Utilitarianism in which the unfortunate were regarded as responsible for their plight.[1] With a genuinely humanitarian impulse, these men did not wish unmarried mothers to die on a blasted heath, take to the streets, or kill their infants; instead, they wanted to restore them to their families and respectability.

Of course, the officials still retained an obsession with female virtue. They recognized working-class reality and accepted a broader definition of chastity encompassing sex after betrothal, defining the ideal applicant as:

> A young woman, having no means of subsistence, except those derived from her own labour, and having no opulent relations, previous to committing the offense bore an irreproachable character, but yielded to artful and long continued seduction, and an express promise of marriage; whose delivery took place in secret, and whose shame was known only to one or two persons, as for example, the medical attendant and a single matron, and lastly, whose employers or other persons were able and desirous to take her into their service, if enabled to earn her livelihood by the reception of the child.[2]

In order to discern if a woman met these qualifications, officials required her to go through three steps. First, she had to submit a petition which revealed the name of her child's father, his occupation, her age, and the child's date of birth. Then, officials would interview the petitioner to ascertain her respectability and the circumstances of her seduction: her employment history, her family, how she met the father, whether he promised marriage, how often and where they had sexual 'connection', why he deserted her, and so on. Finally, they would check the details of her story with her family, friends, and employers. As a result, the factual data from these petitions is quite accurate. Most of the unsuccessful petitioners were rejected for their unsuitable characters, not falsehood, so their testimony gives insight into behaviour not approved of by middle-class authorities.

In order to gain aid from this institution, then, unmarried mothers had to be able to present themselves in conformity with middle-class values. Their class backgrounds ensured some familiarity with bourgeois moral standards, for applicants did not come from the ranks of the very poor. Most sprang from the respectable portions of the working class and the struggling lower middle-class: daughters of sailors, artisans, clerks, small tradesmen, farmers, or the occasional labourer, their mothers took in washing, ran small shops, or assisted in their husbands' businesses. John Gillis has demonstrated the preponderance of servants, especially upper servants, among the petitioners.[3] Some women worked as 'skivvies' or maids of all work in lower middle-class homes or workshops, but petitioners were more likely to wait on guests as parlour maids in West End mansions, assist mistresses as ladies' maids, or suffer the painful ambiguity of governessing.

Other occupations for women in London followed by petitioners were mainly in the clothing trades. While some were the stereotypical sweated needlewomen, driven by starvation to sew shirts for a paltry wage, others were milliners and dressmakers whose lower-middle-class parents wished them to learn a lucrative skill. A few tried to make a living at straw-plaiting, and some teachers even appear in these records.

Whatever their employment, they needed a respectable character to obtain work. Literacy also exposed these women to middle-class moral standards: 77 per cent could sign their names, and even more could read penny-issue novels which featured the dire fate of seduced maidens, or missionaries' tracts about the dangers of passion.

Such women generally followed the traditional courtship customs of their class, obeying community moral standards which allowed sexual intercourse after a solemn promise of marriage. Only their fiancés' desertion prevented them from following 'respectable' lives. If they could present themselves as penitent for a momentary lapse and otherwise chaste, officials of this charity sympathized with their plight, for they most often accepted women who stated they were seduced after betrothal. The contrast between the 70 per cent of accepted petitions which fall into this category, and the 54 per cent of rejected ones who made similar claims, proves the point.

Such sympathy for unmarried mothers had mixed benefits for rape victims who applied to this institution. Seduced women inspired pity for their moral weakness rather than outrage at crimes committed against them. Even if they had been raped, petitioners had to obtain references from their employers or relatives, who could refuse to acknowledge that they were the victims of force rather than their own passion. Women sometimes reported, 'He took advantage of me' in a context which clearly indicated force, but their social superiors misinterpreted their words. A housemaid stated that the footman 'took advantage of her by violence', while her master wrote that the fellow 'has great personal attractions . . . no doubt the fellow took advantage of the petitioner, who is from the country and of simple manners.' Employers over and over stressed that their former servants were truly penitent sinners who atoned for their crimes, ignoring the fact that they had been raped. One wealthy mistress recommended her former lady's maid by stating, 'I believe Henrietta Jackson to be a sincere penitent'; the petitioner had been raped and threatened with death by a courier. Another young woman 'positively stated he accomplished it by force' but her father did not believe her or did not care: he rejected her. In despair, she applied to the Magdalen home for fallen women. In two cases, irate fathers barred their homes to their young daughters who had been raped by their own brothers.[4]

With one exception, officials of this institution were hardly more sympathetic. Before 1834 a claim of rape did not significantly increase a woman's chance of acceptance (a fact which also makes it unlikely women falsely claimed they had been raped). In fact, victims had to make a special effort to assert they had been forced, a difficult task considering the confusion about rape and seduction in both middle- and working-class language. I included in the statistics for rape all those petitions in which a woman said she was 'forced' or claimed she was both 'taken advantage of' or 'seduced' 'against her consent', 'despite her resistance' or 'by violence'. Few women used the more legalistic term 'rape'; because incidences of force were more likely to occur in everyday circumstances they were perceived as immoral rather than criminal.

In 1835 a new official revealed greater sympathy for some rape victims. J.B. Brownlow, a foundling himself, began interviewing petitioners and asking women if they had consented to sexual connection. Before that time, interviewers seem to have asked only where and when petitioners were seduced, and women had to respond that they had been forced without any prompting. The percentage of women claiming they had not consented, or were forced, increased from 15 per cent to 31 per cent of the accepted petitions.

Brownlow, therefore, was more likely to accept women who said they had been raped. His ascendence coincided with

Percentage of petitioners claiming they had been forced 1815–1845

	1815–24	1825–34	1835–45
Accepted:	11.0	15.0	31.0
Rejected:	8.0	14.0	21.0
Total	9.5	14.5	26.0

N = 451 (Accepted), 589 (Rejected), 1040 (All petitioners)

an increasing public belief that unmarried mothers were victims of seduction who yielded out of weakness rather than sexual desire. Like many others, he opposed the unpopular bastardy clauses on the grounds that unmarried mothers were essentially sexless and therefore deserved support.[5] By the 1840s and 1850s, medical experts had begun to promulgate the idea – still rather contentious in the 1830s – that respectable women did not feel sexual arousal.[6] If women were not expected to feel desire, therefore, force and coercion could be paradoxically accepted as normal 'persuasion'. Intercourse could be seen as painful rather than pleasurable as a matter of course, rather than as a result of rape.

The portrayal of unmarried mothers as passive victims intensified the trend of judging women as chaste or unchaste, a trend Brownlow followed. Women who admitted they had consented to sex (especially without promise of marriage) greatly diminished their chances of acceptance, and he believed claims of rape only if the woman had a respectable character and fit the emotional characteristics of the seduced maiden. The women he interviewed had to conform to the role of meek, repentent sinners, even if they had been raped: women with spirit could be rejected with such notations as 'great flippancy of manner and want of feeling'. A woman of good character who said she was persuaded to consent by her fiancé's importunities would be accepted more readily than a woman of uncertain character who claimed a stranger had raped her. For Brownlow, a woman's refusal to consent to sex did not sufficiently prove her chastity, for her chastity was defined not by her own will but by her conformity to patriarchal, middle-class standards of behaviour.

When a woman wrote out her own tale of seduction instead of allowing an interviewer to record it, she almost invariably adopted a tone of melodramatic romance. In fact, this was the only discourse common to working-class and middle-class culture which provided an acceptable explanation for an unmarried mother's plight.

Some of the stories evoke images in melodrama and song of the innocent maiden who *always* faints when ravished. If a woman admitted she had been raped she revealed her loss of the sexual innocence so prized in the early nineteenth-century feminine soul, but if she claimed she fainted, she retained this blissful ignorance and avoided the necessity of describing a confusing and painful experience. Sophie Shepard, raped by the captain of a packetboat on which she sailed from Portsmouth to Plymouth, wrote,

> being very seasick the Captain of the vessel gave her some spirit under pretense of getting rid of the seasickness, by which means your petitioner was reduced to a state of insensibility, and has not knowledge of what happened afterwards.

When she was interviewed, however, she revealed that he had attempted to rape her once before – implying she had been all too conscious of the attack.[7]

Another woman, seduced and abandoned by an attorney, drew upon the melodramatic image of the aristocratic libertine to express her belief in her own chastity and her anger at her own victimization. In a four-page letter replete with clichés about villainous seducers and outraged innocence, Elizabeth Mann apologized for her 'presumption' in writing to appeal the rejection of her petition, explaining 'wounded mental feelings extorts it from me caused by *one of higher rank* but upon whom I look with *disgust* and contempt in his ought-to-be superiority.'[8]

For most women, however, the rhetoric of seduction obscured the difference between rape and seduction. It portrayed women as helplessly yielding to sexual sin, a surrender which tainted them almost irredeemably. Women were always depicted as the victims of sex, but victims of their own weakness in believing perfidious men. This pervasive discourse often prevented women from being able to articulate the difference between rape and seduction. Elizabeth Mann, for instance, could not explain if she had yielded to force or persuasion. Even when officials specifically asked women if they consented, some found it difficult to give a clear answer. One explained, 'she did not consent but did not refuse,' another said, 'connection took place not exactly with her consent but she permitted the consent with some resistance . . . she did not like it.'[9]

The romantic tone of the rhetoric of seduction also contrasted with the reality of women's lives. Very few women were raped by exotic strangers or aristocratic villains – it was hard to fashion a melodramatic tale out of a housemaid's and footman's fumblings in the dark. As John Gillis has shown, the seducers of petitioners to this institution generally resembled them in class status; when they held a higher rank, it was in the lower middle class of tradesmen and clerks.[10] Higher-class men were slightly more likely to use force, but men of the lowest class (porters, labourers, farm servants, and so on) also exhibited a somewhat greater predilection to violence. Masters accounted for only 9 per cent of all rapes reported by petitioners. Fellow servants and lodgers, however, impregnated 34 per cent of petitioners and comprised 44 per cent of the rapists (I will discuss rape in the workplace more fully in the sixth chapter.)

The reality of working-class courtship

The middle-class division of women into chaste and unchaste fundamentally distorted the reality of petitioners' lives. While the bourgeois discourse of seduction regarded both a seduced woman and a rape victim as fundamentally fallen, a different dichotomy guided working women's understanding of sex: either it was a pleasurable act they desired in the context of courtship, or a violent act committed against them. The dilemma of unmarried pregnancy, of course, affected all petitioners equally, but there may have been a significant emotional difference between caring for a child conceived in pleasure and one conceived in pain.

Mundane courtships lead the majority of petitioners into trouble. Eighty-one per cent of the women were impregnated by men who paid them some sort of romantic attention; but 15 per cent of these men raped the women they courted. The majority of women in the sample who said they were forced, in fact, had been victimized by men who courted them. In reality as well as rhetoric, then, seduction sometimes involved force. In order to explain this phenomenon, however, we must understand that premarital sex was quite acceptable among working-class people.

Some women, a minority in this sample, had engaged in rather casual courtships. They 'walked out' with various young men, not necessarily planning on marriage. They went to the theatre, to Greenwich or Gravesend on pleasure excursions, anything to break up the monotony of a servant's life. An even smaller percentage of these women (rarely accepted by officials) engaged in activities regarded by the middle class as prostitution, but by the women themselves as small pleasures purchased with their only valuable possession – their sexuality. Meeting a well-dressed man, they would exchange sexual favours for a treat to the theatre, clothes, or fancy pastries. Some became the mistresses of prosperous artisans, young clerks, or students who would pay for their lodgings; others might occasionally go to the theatre and bagnio (bathhouse) with a new acquaintance. Interestingly enough, most of them did not excuse their activities to the interviewers by claiming they had to chose between sin and starvation. It is possible that women in such desperate situations may have ended up in the workhouse or in the streets rather than applying to this institution.

Most petitioners, however, had more permanent relationships in mind when they indulged in sex outside marriage. High rates of prebridal pregnancy bear witness to the fact that many women who followed this practice eventually married,[11] but formal marriage was not always their goal. Common-law marriages, or merely short-term cohabitation, seem to have been common in certain parts of artisan or rough London, and some women consented if a man merely promised to take care of her should anything happen.[12]

Sexual relationships, whether legal or common-law, were also economic partnerships. These women chose their lovers by carefully considering whether they would be good providers, usually picking respectable working men such as carpenters, shoemakers or tailors.[13] Although most women of the petitioners' type engaged in some sort of productive work after marriage, very few women could earn enough to support themselves and their children, so that support by a man was an economic necessity.

Why did some men rape the women they courted? Rapists did not act out of sexual frustration because women refused them; rather, they refused to acknowledge women's right to desire or refuse themselves, and believed that they had a right to women's bodies. Street ballads continued to promulgate the myth that women say no when they mean yes, as in 'By the Light of the Moon':

> How this fair maid blush'd and grumbled
>> Let me alone, I pray forbear;
> Pray be easy, do not tease me,
>> Touch me again and I'll pull your hair;
> How this fair maid blush'd and grumbled,
>> You have spoiled my gown and new galloon,
> But well pleased my Sally by the light of the moon.[14]

The notion that the conquest of women's resistance was a normal part of sex became even more prevalent in the early nineteenth century. In the eighteenth century, the popular sex manual *Aristotle's Masterpiece* included a little verse from a lover to his mistress, declaring that:

> My Rudder, with thy bold Hand, like a try'd
> And skilful pilot, thou shalt steer, and guide
> My bark in love's dark channel, where it shall
> Dance, as the bounding waves shall rise and fall . . .[15]

But the 1812 version tells the male reader how to overcome his sweetheart's reluctance – or resistance:

> Perhaps when you attempt
> The sweet admission, toyfully she resists;
> With shy reluctance: dauntless you pursue
> The soft attack, and warmly push the war,
> Till quite overpowered with love, the melting maid
> Faintly opposes . . .[16]

Due to the lack of sources about working-class courtship in the eighteenth century, it is impossible to know if this focus on force produced an increased incidence of rape in the early nineteenth century. However, there is much evidence of a 'sexual crisis' in the working class, a crisis which fissured female needs and male expectations.

The traditional courtship pattern functioned well in stable, prosperous times when men and women stayed in the same communities and where marriage was necessary for men to run family farms or artisanal households depending on the labour of wives and children. However, repeated depressions wreaked havoc on working-class families during the early nineteenth century. Years of dearth such as 1816–17 (after the Napoleonic Wars) and the early 1840s saw sharp increases in the number of petitions to this institution from women who would have been able to manage before. Unemployment prevented many men from marrying their pregnant sweethearts.[17]

Especially by the 1830s and 1840s, economic disruption and changing moral ideologies combined to create a situation in which men and women had different interests, values and needs with regard to sex. Barbara Taylor has shown how this sexual crisis led to political conflict in the Owenite socialist movement. Although the Owenite socialists stressed female as well as male desire and repudiated the notion of chastity as property, they went largely unheard, and as Barbara Taylor notes, the male Owenites could not understand and occasionally took advantage of women's sexual vulnerability. In order to defend the working class against the imputations of upper-class moralists, other radicals asserted that working-class women as well as middle-class ladies were pure and sexless.[18]

These petitioners help us see one way in which early nineteenth-century working people played out this crisis in their intimate lives. As Taylor pointed out, deskilling in the London trades meant that skilled craftsmen were reluctant to wed, since they could not support a family and had to move frequently in search of work. In contrast, women desperately needed to marry for economic survival as the range of occupations open to them narrowed to little more than service and sweated needlework or shoebinding.[19] A reputation for chastity was essential to obtain a good character, the recommendation women needed to find places as domestic servants; this made women much less likely to throw caution to the winds. Men, however, faced no such constraints; unable to marry, they often sought sexual pleasure but met with female reluctance.

Many women became enmeshed in the shifting moralities of early nineteenth-century working-class culture as middle-class notions of respectability overtook an older sexual freedom. The class position and literacy of petitioners made this conflict especially confusing for them. Artisans' and tradesmens' daughters learned the older tradition of premarital courtship from their parents and neighbours, while Sunday schools inculcated them with moralistic warnings to retain their chastity. Moral standards changed dramatically within generations: one young woman, reproached by her dying father for living in sin, burst out, 'Don't you know how you brought me up? Don't you remember your drunkenness, and your oaths? how every public house rang with your songs?'[20] Aspirations to respectability contrasted with the harsh conditions of life as a needlewoman or a scullery maid; sex could be a pleasurable escape or a path to ruin, how was a woman to know? Domestic servants in particular were exposed to contradictory moralities, growing up in plebeian neighbourhoods while witnessing the luxuries of bourgeois life at work.

Women's expectations of sexual pleasure may have faded by the 1830s and 1840s, when courtship tended to be a route to survival rather than enjoyment. They may have known less about sex as well: *Aristotle's Masterpiece*, no longer published information that eighteenth-century versions had included on the female genitalia and role of the clitoris.[21] Furthermore, by the 1840s women were all too eager to cash in their sexual value for the security of marriage.[22]

The men who courted these women also faced a confusing variety of moral standards, but they did not have to live with the consequences of an unlucky choice. Men faced diminished moral pressure from their communities to treat women well. Female servants concealed their liaisons to avoid the 'no followers' rule, but as Gillis notes mistresses and relatives could not then pressure errant lovers into marriage.[23] The bastardy clauses of the 1834 New Poor Law freed men from their previous responsibility to maintain illegitimate children, benefiting working-class men but forcing poor unmarried mothers into prison-like workhouses.

Some men refused to promise marriage until after a woman consented to sex, following older customs, and turned their resentment at rejection into violence; others, following bourgeois morality, believed that a woman who consented before marriage would be an unfaithful wife, but tested her virtue by attempting to seduce her or even raping her.[24] There is also evidence that men may have forced women who refused to consent to sex without promise of marriage. Only 10.5 per cent of men who promised marriage were reported to have raped their fiancées, but of women who had been courted without a promise, 38 per cent of successful petitioners, and 20 per cent of rejected petitioners reported they had been forced.

For men who more readily accepted bourgeois morality, rape could be seen as a regrettable loss of control rather than a criminal act, as moralists continually presented passion as a force which could only be brought under control with great difficulty. After raping Eliza Fanshaw, a cook he was courting, a blacksmith wrote,

> Expression wrongs my love and it would need no other but this paper to convince you of the Purity your love hath made in me and long doth the time seem to be parted from you I would have come down but knowing that I am not fit to come to the house i thought it best to keep away.[25]

Eliza Fanshaw did not accept his apologies; his passion seemed like violence to her. There were two strategies available to women who were the victims of rape: silence or protest. Some women resigned themselves to courtship after rape in hopes of marriage, as Gillis has noted. For instance, in 1823 housemaid Sally Swarthmore stated that her sweetheart, a footman, crept into her bedroom and had 'criminal conversation' with her; the next morning 'She taxed him with his conduct . . he again promised to take care of her and from this time she gave herself up to him with the expectation he would marry her.'[26]

Most women in these petitions, of course, did not express ambivalent feelings; many reacted to rape in an unequivocally negative manner. The lover of twenty-three-year-old Mary Thornton, a woman who lived at home with her blind sister, lured her into a strange house under the pretense it was the house of a friend. What happened there she did not say, but afterwards, 'She told him never to see her again, she was so disgusted with his conduct.'[27] After Mary Carr was violently raped by a farm labourer who worked for her father, she told him 'she was very sorry for what he had done – he said he was sorry too and again promised to marry her but she told him she had lost all affection for him.'[28]

Whether she had been raped or seduced, the unmarried mother faced the same dire plight. But the fact that so many women were raped by men who courted them could only have intensified their emotional trauma.

Conclusion

As we have seen, the reality of unmarried mothers' lives differed dramatically from the image of the seduced maiden. They were not tainted by sin, but victims of circumstances beyond their control. But the rhetoric of seduction was so pervasive that it sometimes distorted women's ability to articulate and protest their experiences of rape, as well as imparting a sense of shame to those who had enjoyed sexual pleasure. These middle-class discourses could not help them face the real sexual crisis within the working class. Yet radical rhetoric could not help them either; as the next chapter will show, by placing the responsibility for sexual exploitation on the shoulders of aristocrats and factory owners, it evaded the fact that working-class men accounted for most violence inflicted against working-class women.

CHAPTER 6

The daughters of poor men: radical rhetoric, women's experience

In the early nineteenth century, the image of the innocent but poor maiden seduced and abandoned by an aristocratic libertine came to serve as a powerful metaphor for the exploitation of the poor by the rich. Originated by the Jacobin novelists of the late eighteenth century who attributed every vice to aristocratic villains, this image was borrowed by radicals from melodrama and penny-issue novels.[1] Bradford anti-Poor Law activist Peter Bussey directly linked economic with sexual exploitation when he claimed, 'There is a set of young boobies in this country, who are connected with the aristocracy, and who are regular plunderers of the people; they seek your blood, but you are useful in labouring for them. This brood are on the increase, and they are in the habit of seducing the daughters of poor men . . .'[2] An Owenite socialist declared, 'The vile aristocracy . . . seduce and abandon more girls than all the other male population put together.'[3]

Was this image any closer to the reality of sexual victimization than the charitable discourse of the pitiful seduced maiden? It did question the behaviour of the seducer, rather than of his victim. And upper-class men could rape women with a degree of impunity because they were unlikely to be reported, let alone convicted; their female subordinates could rarely protest against sexual assault. Economic power also enabled them to coerce women into sexual acquiescence by threatening to discharge them, and they could buy sex from needy women. For them, rape could be seen as an extension of their economic power, a reinforcement of their already dominant position as upperclass and male.

The growth of large institutions associated with the development of industrial capitalism also provided new opportunities for rape in the early nineteenth century. Women and children were vulnerable to sexual assault by the masters and staff of greatly expanded mental asylums, prisons, and workhouses, and contemporary observers identified factory work as a crucial site of the economic and sexual exploitation of women and children.[4] In London, sweated needlework establishments were subject to the same accusations.[5] All these institutions intensified the power of male masters and supervisors over large numbers of young females, power rarely mitigated by familial ties.

The impact of the image of the seduced maiden, however, derived less from any resemblance to the reality of upper-class violence than from its ability to simplify the problems working-class people faced into one emotive symbol. During the early nineteenth century, industrialization and recurrent depressions disrupted traditional family economies. In the North, factories displaced male handloom weavers; children and wives went into the mills instead of working under the patriarchal roof. London sweatshops exploited the cheap labour of women and children and also undermined the status of skilled male artisans. The subsequent unemployment led many skilled men to abandon their pregnant sweethearts, exacerbating the trauma of illegitimacy. While the image of the seduced maiden thus reflected generalized anxieties about the effect of economic exploitation on families, it distorted the reality of sexual assault as experienced by working-class women and children.

By focusing on the sexual exploitation of young females, radicals could see the problem of women's work as one of morality, rather than labour, and the solution as the removal of wives and daughters back into the home.[6] The home, however, posed much greater sexual danger than the factories. Women and children continued to face most sexual assault from men of their own class, who could be acquaintances, relatives, or fellow workers.

To examine the possible effects of industrial capitalism on the problem of sexual assault, three factors must be considered: motive, immunity, and opportunity. The first question is the most difficult, for it is impossible to state exactly how the industrial revolution did or did not motivate rapists. However, if we proceed from the assumption that rape stems from the desire to dominate women, the effect of social change on this desire can be examined. Industrial capitalism intensified the power of male employers over female workers while proletarian men lost some of their control over women of their own class. Yet proletarian men could still attempt to dominate women within the contexts of popular amusements, the family, and the workplace. This is not to say that capitalism *caused* these assaults: rather, while capitalism may have caused a feeling of powerlessness or intensified power, patriarchy created the justification for taking it out on females and regarding female sexuality as a thing to be taken. Since many or most rapes seem to have been planned, the assailant must also have believed he would have immunity from punishment. The judicial treatment of men accused of rape, and the bastardy clauses which exonerated men from responsibility for their illegitimate children, indicated an immunity from punishment for sexual exploitation which cut across class lines. Changes in the workplace could also affect opportunities for sexual assault; a rapist required proximity to a victim who was isolated from others who could have aided her.

The vulnerability of female factory hands, children, and domestic servants to sexual exploitation aroused great concern in the early nineteenth century; by examining the empirical evidence of sexual assault on these females, this chapter will assess the effects of the Industrial Revolution on motives and opportunities for rape.

Sexual assault in the textile industry

The factory system aroused intense hatred for its perceived disruption of the traditional artisan family economy. Radicals attacked not only the long hours and meagre pay for which young millhands worked; they reserved especial ire for the factory owners who supposedly took advantage of their position to rape innocent factory girls. In the penny-issue novel *The Factory Lad* (1834), Thorneycraft, 'a heartless cotton lord' inflicts his 'monstrous lust' on an 'unyielding, resisting victim', the pauper Sally.[7] The great Tory Radical Richard Oastler declared in 1831, 'I know that there are scenes of the grossest prostitution amongst the poor creatures who are victims of the system, and in some cases, they are objects of the cruelty and rapacity and sensuality of the masters.'[8]

In reality, factory girls faced more immediate danger of rape by overlookers and other male workers than lordly, distant masters. Children, who started working in the mills at the beginning of the century, were thought to be particularly vulnerable to assaults. In Chester, a judge commented in 1824 that rapes of children were an 'all-too common vice . . above all, in this manufacturing country, where the females were, at a tender age, placed away from the control of their parents, to work at the factories.'[9] Violence against children was indeed endemic in the mills.[10] Adult spinners employed children to piece broken yarn for them; while women enticed their charges to work long hours with sweet talk and small bribes, male spinners were notorious for beating young boys and girls.[11] This violence occasionally extended to sexual assault. C.R. James, a linen weaver, in 1821 raped several small girls who wound bobbins in the Leeds workshop which employed him.[12] In 1822, a Carlisle weaver named Horsely raped the thirteen-year-old girl who put the web in his loom; interestingly enough he successfully excused his assault by alleging the girl solicited him with lascivious language, thus drawing upon the stereotype of the immoral working girl. John Holmes, a clothdresser, raped several little girls in his workplace in 1821, although it is not clear if they were employed there.[13]

No cases of adult women assaulted in factories or mills are found in the assize depositions up until 1829, since women only began working there in the 1830s, but the newspapers reported three incidents of young girls raped by overseers between 1830 and 1845. Benjamin Haywood, an aged man, was fined five pounds for an indecent assault on a girl who worked in the Hunslet cotton mill where he was employed as an overlooker. If he had been a poor man, he would have been imprisoned for two months in default of the fine.[14] Jeptha Paver, a thirty-four-year-old married man, was an overlooker in a flax mill who raped Eliza Higgins, a fifteen-year-old factory girl, but he was found not guilty when tried at the assizes.[15] The apparent immunity of these overlookers from punishment for their sexual crimes excited public outrage. James Blakesley, a Bradford overlooker, not only raped but impregnated a little girl of fourteen whom he superintended, yet magistrates did not feel there was enough evidence to commit him for trial. Though he was dismissed from his post, local people were not satisfied with this decision; Blakesley narrowly escaped a mauling by the crowd, 'who pursued him to a considerable distance, with the loudest shouts and vociferations.'[16]

It is possible that many overlookers escaped punishment for the sexual abuse of girls who worked under them because of the shortage of magistrates in rapidly growing factory towns. Parents of millgirls frequently complained that when their children were assaulted, they could not find magistrates to whom they could submit complaints.[17]

When working men themselves (as opposed to politicians such as Oastler) testified to factory commissioners about the day-to-day dangers of women's and children's work in the mills, assaults by overlookers and masters comprised only part of the attacks of which they told. Newspaper reports bore out their assertions that mill girls faced the danger of sexual assault as they travelled home from work. In this case it was the moral contagion of women's work outside the home rather than direct attacks by upper-class men which aroused working-class anxieties. The Reverend G.S. Bull, a Bradford Tory radical, testified that 'in their returning home from their work, the elder of young females especially are . . . very frequently decoyed and seduced.'[18] As Mary Thornton and several other Bradford power-loom weavers made their way home one evening across Eccleshill Moor, Samuel Jaggar 'came out of the Spotted Cow beershop . . . in a state of intoxication, and immediately laid hold of a girl of the company, and used her in a very improper manner.'[19] Thomas Spink, seventeen, and George Johnson, eighteen, seized two carders from a Leeds factory as they played together after work; they dragged them into a nearby field and raped them.[20]

Evidence from newspapers and court records, then, bolstered the fears working people expressed about the sexual dangers inherent in factory work. But as the factory commission witnesses told of the rapes, harassments, and assaults their daughters and sisters endured in the mills, they also stressed the immorality factory work engendered in young females. These men, who worked in the mills themselves, testified that, 'both sexes take great familiarities with each other in the mills, without being ashamed of their conduct.'[21] William Kershaw, a Leeds man, said 'impudence and immorality of every description' characterized his millgirl daughters.[22] Mathew Crabtree, also of Leeds, was horrified at the indecent language and bawdy jokes children used to keep themselves awake, and John Hannan even alleged that factory girls had access to information about abortion.[23] Francis Place, a well-known working-class radical, claimed that in factories 'girls are willingly debauched at 12 years of age.'[24]

These accusations suggest that working-class anxiety about the sexual dangers of factory work may have derived more from their intense hatred of the factory system than from any real increase in sexual violence. The factories, with their intimidating machinery, rigid timetables, and domination of the landscape, threatened not only the livelihood but the self-respect of textile artisans. However, when the presence of females in factories was seen by male workers as a moral danger in itself, they were less likely to focus on the very real economic exploitation women faced. Although young women were often ready and eager to strike, many men saw the solution to their hardships as the withdrawal of female labour from factories rather than trade union organization and a living wage for women.[25]

Despite the immense hardship of long hours, low pay, lethal accidents, and alienating labour, factory girls may have faced less danger of actual rape than other working women, although they certainly contended with a level of sexual harassment. In a study of Manchester, David Phillips found 'few sexual assaults at the place of work . . . despite the obvious readiness of contemporaries like Peter Gaskell to seek it out.'[26] Overlookers certainly had the power to force girls into sex, but in large mills with hundreds of workers they would have had relatively few opportunities to surprise their victims unawares. The very coarse language and sexual knowledge of which male workers complained could enable young girls to resist and protest against sexual assault more openly.

Factory girls were notorious for working and travelling in large, boisterous groups, singing and shouting and always ready for a fight. Their solidarity would enable them to fend off attackers, making them less vulnerable than women who worked alone in isolated homes and fields. When Samuel Jaggar, as noted above, assaulted several power loom weavers, one girl 'struck him with all the force she could over the face' so he would free her friend.[27] Harriet Dunwell cried out to her companions, 'Lasses, come and help me,' and Alice Varey ran to her aid, shouting 'Let her go!' when Thomas Spink and George Jackson attacked them.[28] Although their resistance was not successful, the fact that they fought back so vigorously may indicate that many other women were able to help repel sexual attacks.

Factory work, then, was seen as introducing new moral perils, but women continued to be more vulnerable to sexual assault outside the mills – in agricultural work and in the home. Traditional male working-class amusements, for instance, posed more danger to women than the new institution of factory work. While factory girls comprised only 4 per cent of victims of rape in newspaper reports, gang rapes accounted for 13 per cent of rapes between 1830 and 1845.

Male bonding augmented men's physical power over women, a power available to even the poorest men. Gang rapes were almost exclusively committed by youths – 74 per cent were committed by those aged twenty and under. Although both radical and Tory newspapers reported them as 'shameful outrages' they were not strange deviations but actions firmly rooted in the traditional culture of young men. Gang rape was a ritualistic proof of masculinity, an adolescent rite of passage, growing out of seemingly more innocuous amusements of Yorkshire youth. Joseph Lawson wrote that in the textile village of Pudsey, 'It was common for young men to stand in certain places at land ends . . . playing at pitch and toss . . . singing sometimes indelicate songs . . . or worse still, in making audible personal remarks about single or married women who might pass.'[29]

These young men did not always restrict their harassment to drunken, rude remarks. For instance, as shoebinder Jane Milnes rode in a cart from Bradford to Leeds, she knew trouble was in store when she passed a public house where twenty young men were gathered outside, using 'very bad language'. Six of them followed the cart, jumped into it, and dragged her into a field where one raped her.[30] Assailants seemed to have planned gang rapes, hanging around country lanes until a likely victim walked by. In an 1829 case, fifteen-year-old Ralph Fisher testified that he was walking with some young men through fields when 'a girl came by, Sheppard said that is a country girl he would go and take care of her . . .'. Gang rape was one way men could prove themselves to each other, or indirectly humiliate other men. For instance, Thomas Dowling and two companions (all woolcombers) raped a co-worker's wife in front of him after a drunken quarrel.[31]

Sexual assault on children

The labour of children outside their own families became a crucial issue in the early nineteenth century. While child labour was certainly not new, their work in the large, regimented, impersonal textile mills aroused great public concern, and sexual abuse exemplified the dangers they faced there. For middle-class reformers, children were to be kept innocent and pure in the domestic shelter of the family, while for Northern textile workers, the economic exploitation of their children was the worst cruelty industrial capitalism could inflict.

During the period when children began to work in factories, there was a startling increase in the number of cases of assaults on children in the North-east Assize records. While sexual assaults on girls under thirteen accounted for only 2 per cent of the depositions in the late eighteenth century assize records, they provide 27 per cent of the depositions from 1800 to 1829, and 30 per cent of the sexual assaults reported in the northern newspapers between 1830 and 1845 involve children. Furthermore, researchers today have found that most sexual abuse of children does not involve physical violence or even intercourse;[32] if this was so in the early nineteenth century, the court records vastly underestimate the incidence of such abuse since the assize courts only dealt with rape and attempted rape. However, it is also likely that the increase in assize cases represents growing concern with the problem rather than a higher incidence; cases which, in the eighteenth century may have been dealt with by the quarter sessions, may have been judged in the higher courts in the later period.

And the sexual assault of children, like the victimization of their older sisters, cannot be explained as the result of the factory system. While in the North-east, skilled workers such as weavers, joiners, tailors and blacksmiths accounted for a disproportionate number of these assailants – 83 per cent in the newspaper sample and 59 per cent in assize depositions – only six of the attacks took place in mills or workshops.

Most sexual assaults of children took place in homes and neighbourhoods, for urban areas may have provided assailants with more victims among the children who played in the streets while their mothers struggled to make a living. Crowded living conditions may have increased the vulnerability of children to sexual abuse,[33] for itinerant skilled workers often lived in lodgings, sometimes sharing a room with a family where they had access to their landlady's children. John Pellitt, a Keighley tailor, raped seven-year-old Mary

Ann Nicholls in his bed even though John Dickinson, a woolcombmaker, was sleeping in the same room.[34] Parish children, farmed out with little care by Poor Law officials, were especially vulnerable to such attacks. Ann Shaw, only seven, was first raped by her mother's lover and then by Edward Locksmith, a blacksmith whose wife had taken her in.[35]

A disproportionate number of old men and young boys attacked female children, but there were many married and middle-aged assailants. In fact, in one case a wife was aware of her husband's designs on little neighbourhood girls, but as she worked in a Stockport factory she could not prevent him from luring them to the house.[36]

While proximity gave these men the opportunity to rape little girls, it is difficult to understand why skilled craftsmen in particular would be motivated to do so. Artisans were undergoing deskilling at this time; one could speculate that they compensated for their loss of economic power by exerting power over young females. However, this is an incomplete explanation, for London skilled artisans, who were also undergoing this process, were not overrepresented as assailants of little girls, and there is no particular evidence of a great increase in child assault in the capital. Out of ninety-three men accused of sexually assaulting children whose occupations were given in the newspaper reports (a problematic source, but the only one available) 32 per cent were from the ranks of the labouring poor, 18 per cent skilled artisans, 10 per cent apprentices, 21 per cent lower-middle-class (shopkeepers, schoolmasters and so on) and 18 per cent middle and upper class (officers, 'gentlemen', professionals, merchants).

Forty per cent of the fathers of victims in the newspaper sample were from the lower-middle class; it is possible that poorer parents were less likely to report the sexual abuse of their daughters. As in the eighteenth century, many such cases (ten, or 11 per cent) involved an apprentice assaulting his master's daughter, reversing the usual dynamic of master-servant exploitation. As in the North-east, a large proportion (47 per cent of those whose ages were given) were described as 'old', fitting a popular stereotype of child molesters.

Men of genteel backgrounds seem over-represented in the newspaper reports, although this may be due to the *Weekly Dispatch's* tendency to denounce aristocratic sexual vice as emblematic of class exploitation. Disturbingly, there is some evidence that the assault of female children by elite men may have been encouraged by expensive pornography and catered to by procurers of child prostitutes, as the following passage from an erotic journal indicates. *The New Rambler's Magazine* described a nine-year-old girl procured by an old woman for a wealthy, aged officer:

> The child had an appearance of modesty, but it was only in appearance; she had been tainted by the foul company she kept in the metropolis, and was willing to be bad, as a bad man could make her . . . . The little girl cried loudly every time the gentleman made free with her little person; but she was not in the least averse to his caresses.[37]

While ostensibly condemning such assaults, the magazine actually excused them and even heightened their erotic appeal by portraying the child as depraved and interpreting the child's pain and resistance as compliance.

Men who did not wish to pay for their victims could find them on the London streets, running errands or peddling old clothes; contemporary observers often noted the swarms of children who played and worked there, sometimes pitying them, sometimes deploring their penchant to petty crime. John Clarke, a surveyor of Chelsea, was caught by a constable as he assaulted an eleven-year-old girl in a dark alley,[38] and a clergyman lured a young child to a 'secluded part of Covent Garden market, where he took improper liberties and proposed to accompany her to a house in the neighbourhood' which was notorious for its many brothels.[39] But labouring men also victimized poor children. Sarah Lewis, a seven-year-old-child, was sent out on an errand by her father, a weaver, when a 'rough-looking Irishman' knocked her down and attempted to rape her in a drunken fit.[40]

It cannot be assumed that most sexual assaults on children were committed by strangers in workplaces, crowded lodgings, or dark alleys. A small number of cases of incest occur in the newspapers and assize depositions, and no doubt these were the most underreported sexual assaults of all. Out of 138 cases of sexual assaults of girls under thirteen reported in my sample of London newspapers between 1800 and 1845, eighteen involved incest. Thirteen more incest cases were reported involving girls over twelve, the age of consent. Although this is a very small sample, it is important to discuss the issue, for researchers today have found that the vast majority of girls who have been sexually abused were victimized by relatives or family friends.[41]

The assailants, mostly fathers and stepfathers, included four labourers, two watermen, a master weaver, a sawyer, a cabinet-maker, a shipwright, a soldier, a poulterer, a hairdresser, a silversmith and jeweller, two shoemakers, an accountant, and a preacher. There were four cases in the assize records from the North-east: one father was a farmer, another a knifemaker or seller, and the other two unknown. While middle- and upper-class men were no doubt less likely to be accused publicly of this crime, the skilled craftsmen and tradesmen in the sample seemed quite prosperous. Therefore, incest cannot automatically be described as the result of social disorganization and anomie caused by industrialization. In their historical study of nineteenth- and early twentieth-century Boston, Gordon and O'Keefe found that incestuous fathers were no less stressed than men who committed other types of more common family violence.[42]

Obviously, only those cases in which the girl was brave, strong, and old enough to prosecute, or when a neighbour, mother, or sister interfered, would be brought to court, and such circumstances were rare.[43] For instance, the wife of Abraham Angell, a silversmith and jeweller, gave him into custody after he assaulted their daughter; twelve years old, she had been rescued by her sisters.[44] In Yorkshire, Sarah Inglefor separated from her husband and prosecuted him after she found he had raped two of their daughters.[45]

Present-day analysts have described incestuous fathers as despotic and extremely patriarchal; while they may have felt a sense of failure in the outside world, they wished to exercise total control over their families. The mothers were often ill, weak, or victimized themselves, and therefore unable to rescue their daughters.[46] Given the fact that the incestuous abuse by many of these fathers was only part of the violence they inflicted on their wives and daughters, many women were afraid to report their husbands. It must be remembered in this context that until 1839 fathers had absolute custody rights over their offspring, no matter how cruelly they had abused their wives and children.[47] William Bewsher, a Cumberland farmer, turned his wife out of doors one morning and then raped his seventeen-year-old daughter Elizabeth, and had also raped his eleven-year-old daughter Mary months before. Their mother deposed that 'the reason for her concealing the circumstances, was the fear of an injury from her said husband – for that from her having told of his ravishing her Elder daughter Elizabeth about four years since, he had beaten her excessively and threatened to kill her.'[48]

In several cases, incestuous fathers seemed to have regarded their children as substitutes for their wives, a pattern often noted in contemporary incest cases and in Gordon and O'Keefe's historical study.[49] After the wife of William Partis, a shipwright, died, he took his twelve-year-old daughter to bed and violated her twice; he also had 'ill-used' an older sister.[50] In Marylebone, Edward Leader, thirty-five, raped his ten-year-old daughter first when her mother was confined and several times afterwards; his son, a 'respectable tradesman', testified that Leader had 'much neglected his wife'. Leader had to be conveyed to Newgate in a cab, 'with a view of preventing any riot or outrage . . . so great was the indignation of the public against the perpetrator of so abominable a crime.'[51]

Incest was clearly disapproved of publicly, but the men who committed it did not often regard it as a crime. While one Bury bricklayer killed himself when his wife discovered the abuse of her daughter, none of the other accused men evinced any remorse.[52] In 1823 a cabinet-maker named Joseph Wilson went so far as to tell his nineteen-year-old daughter that her resistance to his indecent solicitations 'was in observance of the tyrant law of custom, and that it was not against the law of nature.' Despite this excuse, he was sentenced to twenty months hard labour.[53] When a shoemaker named Barry was brought before a magistrate charged with the attempted rape of his fifteen-year-old daughter, he 'listened to the charge with the utmost indifference, and frequently laughed.'[54] Since incest was only illegal if the child was under thirteen, some men tried to claim their victims had consented.[55] A man named Upton was acquitted for the rape of his thirteen-year-old daughter on such grounds, but Edward Eldridge's claim that his stepdaughter consented in order to obtain new clothes was less successful – he was committed to trial.[56] The fact that only twelve out of twenty-five London incestuous assailants were biological fathers (nine were stepfathers, the others uncles, a grandfather, and a brother) may provide one reason for such lack of remorse. As Gordon and O'Keefe note, while stepfathers played the social role of father, they may have felt less committment to the child, and therefore 'less empathy with the distress they caused their victims'.[57]

While magistrates and judges viewed such cases with horror, they did not always punish incestuous fathers or stepfathers. In one, perhaps symptomatic case, a magistrate declared, 'it would be better, perhaps, though the monster ought not to go unpunished, that the public feeling should not be wounded by the disgusting details' necessarily exposed in a trial.[58] Only one of four men accused of incestuous rape in the North-east assize depositions between 1800 and 1829 was found guilty. At the conclusion of the trial of William Townsley for raping his eleven-year-old daughter, Mr Justice Bayley admitted that the child had proven the assault, but recommended acquittal because the only other corroborating evidence was the mother, who 'in point of law, could not give evidence against her husband . . . for those wise reasons that domestic divisions or family differences might induce her to state an untruth to the prejudice or injury of her husband.'[59] Incest was thus a crime too bound up in the patriarchal family to punish consistently; from what little evidence we have, however, its prevalence cannot be attributed to the anomie of the industrial revolution.

Danger in the domestic sphere

In the early nineteenth century, the labour of women in factories, fields, or streets excited contemporary fears of sexual exploitation, but the majority of women continued to labour at home, as servants if not wives and mothers. Although the ideology of separate spheres promised women protection if they stayed in such traditional roles, they faced considerable danger of sexual assault in the home. The assize depositions from 1800 to 1829 show that 32 per cent of victims were raped in their own homes or the houses where they worked as domestic servants. Servants accounted for 53 per cent of the victims of rape in the assize records, and 26 per cent in the northern newspapers. The records of the London charitable institution also reveal that most petitioners who were raped were servants.

Servants occupied a somewhat anomalous position, for they worked within the home in a very feminine occupation, but they were not 'family' and their work was heavy and dirty. As Liz Stanley notes, by the early nineteenth century service had become in some ways a 'total institution' like the factory or workhouse: domestics were depersonalized, regimented, their lives subject to total control by their employers.[60] Nonetheless, it must be noted that most servants had to deal with their employers directly, on a one-to-one level. This peculiar combination of class subordination embedded in a personal relationship made servants particularly vulnerable to sexual assault. Unlike factory workers, they often lacked the support or even presence of other female workers to protect them, and their chastity was of paramount importance in retaining the 'character' so essential in finding a place.

The rape of a maid by a master is an enduring stereotype of nineteenth-century class exploitation, an image which still has the capacity to provoke anger at the hypocrisy of the Victorian patriarch who publicly denounced working-class morality but privately molested his housemaid. The *Northern Star*, a Chartist newspaper, delighted in reprinting accounts of bastardy examinations or rape trials about servants victimized by their employers.

In the North-east assize depositions, rapes by masters or masters' relatives increased from 9 per cent in the late eighteenth century to 19 per cent between 1800 and 1829. The availability of textile work may have increased the willingness of servants to prosecute their masters by providing an alternative source of employment, for contemporary observers often noted that Yorkshire girls preferred factory work to service.[61] This change may also have been related to shifts in the lifestyle and composition of households which employed servants in the North-east. Traditionally, both male and female servants lived in as part of the household, eating their meals with farmers' families; with the gentrification of some farmers, the male labourers began to live out and female servants aided the farmer's wife in her quest to become a lady.[62] In the cities, industrialism brought with it a new middle class of tradesmen and professionals who required female servants to maintain the gentility of their homes. However, these masters were not the aristocratic young boobies of the lurid myth of seduction, but more often well-off artisans or tradesmen who retained a familiarity with their servants. Francis Poutry, a Leeds gardener, offered his servant Mary Ann Rawson a shilling if she would let him kiss her in the shop, but she 'told him to give over and be ashamed of himself.'[63] Elizabeth Senthouse was raped by her master's son, a labourer who had flirted with her and asked if she wished to be married.[64]

In contrast, there is no evidence of an increase in the incidence of rape by masters on their servants in London since the eighteenth century. The newspapers are a completely unreliable source for these incidences, as both Yorkshire and London newspapers report very low percentages of master-servant assaults, no doubt due to the ability of middle-class men to bribe reporters to ignore their appearances before magistrates.

The records of the London charitable institution, however, also reveal quite a low percentage of master-servant rape:

these incidents account for only 9 per cent of all rapes reported by petitioners, most of whom were servants. To speculate on the possible reasons for the disparity between Yorkshire and London, it is possible that masters may have seduced women through bribes and promises of support; even while they felt exploited, women would thus be less likely to report their masters to the authorities and have less need of charitable aid. Theodore Boulet, a prosperous French basket maker, seduced his fifteen-year-old servant and placed her into lodgings, a fact which came to light when her enraged father assaulted him.[65] Mr George Wood, a gentleman who resided near Hyde Park, charged Mary Carton with ringing his bell and annoying him, but she claimed she had borne two children to him while in his service, and needed more than the ten shillings a week he paid her.[66]

An alternative explanation could be that some female servants may have been more on their guard against masters than fellow servants if they felt any kind of physical contact with masters would not only be dangerous but would not lead to a relationship. Many did not even accept minor liberties from masters: when Elizabeth Smith charged Mr Kelsey, a lodging housekeeper who employed her as a housemaid, with placing his arm around her waist and attempting to embrace her, the magistrate at Marlborough Street ordered him to find bail.[67] Isabella Roberts, aged fourteen, complained at the Marylebone Office that Mr Cornelius Hancock, a fruiterer, had tried to kiss her while she poured out his tea, and then discharged her when she told her mother. Hancock tried to excuse himself in court, explaining, 'I owe there was some little liberty taken, I pulled her on my knee and kissed her . . . but . . . she is a very loose girl . . .', but the magistrate ordered him to find bail for the offence.[68] When a friend of her master offered to kiss and molest her, Hannah Cullwick successfully repulsed him by threatening to do something which would hurt him if he tried.[69]

Petitioners tended to be upper servants employed in elaborate households where male servants also worked. Unlike the cheesemongers or joiners who appear most often in these statistics as violent masters, the masters of these large households may have felt a mild taboo on sexual relationships with lower-class servants. The physical division of homes into servant quarters and the employers' chambers by long corridors and stairs accentuated this psychological distance, which as Leonore Davidoff writes derived from the association of servants with dirt and degradation.[70] Of course, for bourgeois men this taboo contributed to the allure of servants as objects of desire in pornographic fantasy, but from a servant's point of view she actually faced greater danger of rape from other men in her employers' household.

As in the case of violence against women and children in the factories, class was only one form of power which men could use to exploit women sexually. Some masters certainly did rape their servants, but servants faced most danger of attack from men of similar social status. Lodgers committed 14 per cent of the rapes on petitioners and fellow servants 31 per cent. Serving in large households, small businesses, shops, boarding houses, and pubs, the men servants encountered most often were not their masters or other upper-class men but footmen, butlers, journeymen, shop assistants, customers, and medical students, clerks, or artisans in lodgings.

Lodgers and male servants shared with masters three factors which gave them the power to assault female servants. Aside from physical force, they derived both opportunity to rape and impunity from punishment from the peculiar circumstances of women's servitude. Women were more likely to be friendly with, or even courting, the male servants they worked with, so they would not be as cautious in avoiding dangerous situations. As John Gillis has written, male servants who courted petitioners sometimes raped them, perhaps because cooks and parlourmaids were reluctant to consent to sex with a man of lower-class status when an advantageous marriage could not result.[71]

But lodgers, masters, and male servants could also surprise women as they worked alone in a house, assaulting a servant as she brought hot water to a bedroom or cleaned isolated parlours. Fellow servants seemed especially prone to creeping into a maid's bedroom late at night or assaulting her as she worked in the kitchen while the rest of the household was out. A waiter at the pub where Susan Black worked had often tried to 'take liberties with her' and one night he 'went to her bed in the middle of the night and forced her . . . she left him as soon as she could and sat on the stairs for two hours . . . the next morning she told her mistress who laughed at her.'[72] Parlour maid Mary Lexington said a medical student lodger 'forced her criminally when he came in late at night and she was waiting up.'[73]

Lodgers, masters, and male servants all knew that they were unlikely to suffer any consequences from their violent behaviour, for women hesitated to protest to their mistresses; they risked being sacked for immorality themselves. An accusation of rape branded the victim herself as 'unchaste', spoiling her 'character' which was so necessary for employment.

The radical emphasis on the sexual exploitation of women by masters ignored the fact that in a way, lower-class men were their masters too.[74] Female servants' peculiar vulnerability to rape stemmed from their position in the patriarchal household as well as their class position. Like middle-class wives and daughters, domestic servants were isolated within the home, and their place there depended on their chastity, while their subordinate position intensified their vulnerability to sexual assault from masters and fellow servants.

Conclusion

For the quintessential working females of the early nineteenth century – millgirls, child labourers and domestic servants – class exploitation only partially explained their sexual vulnerability. The new work situations of the Industrial Revolution – the middle-class household, the mill, the use of child labour – provided new opportunities for men to sexually assault females, but they did not provide the motive. Masters and overlookers could rape female workers with impunity, due to their control over their victims' employment, but adult men of all classes had the power of sex and adulthood over children of their own class. Young men, no matter how lowly their economic position, drew upon the power of the male bonding to commit gang rapes on women young and old. Male servants took advantage of their proximity to female domestics in order to inflict violence upon them. A few fathers abused their patriarchal power and incestuously assaulted their daughters.

For all these men, no matter what class they belonged to, rape was a means by which they could gain a sense of their own power by humiliating and degrading individual women. These men derived their power – and their immunity from punishment for its abuse – from the structures of male power over all women: an economy in which a woman's sexuality was her most valuable possession; a religion which enshrined chastity as the measure of a woman's worth; and a legal system which protected all men who committed violence against women. Like the discourses of charity officials, doctors, and judges, the radical image of the seduced maiden distorted the reality of women's experience with its patriarchal concern for women's virtue.

While this chapter has shown that the blame for actual sexual assaults of working-class women and children cannot be placed solely on class exploitation, the next chapter will demonstrate that the myth of rape as a warning to women did arise from middle-class attempts to control the streets.

CHAPTER 7

Rape as warning: the genesis of a middle-class myth

> As a warning to female virtue, and an humble monument
> to female chastity, this Stone marks the grave of Mary
> Ashford, who in the 20th year of her age, having
> incautiously repaired to a scene of amusement, without
> proper protection, was brutally violated and murdered on
> 27th May, 1817.[1]

Mary Ashford was a young servant who apparently met her
death at the hands of Abraham Thornton, a bricklayer, near
Birmingham. The huge controversy aroused by his acquittal
marks the beginning of a myth which haunts women to this
day: that women who take their freedom for granted will be
punished by rape, while women who stay at home will be
safe. This myth arose out of the efforts of bourgeois moralists
to impose their restrictive standards of behaviour on all
women, confining them to their place under patriarchal
control.

Women in the eighteenth century certainly had reason to
fear rape, but they were vulnerable to sexual assault
everywhere, not just in public space. The myth of rape as
warning arose in the 1810s and 1820s out of two related
historical developments: the ideology of separate spheres and
the suppression of working-class street culture.

For middle-class women, the new ideology of separate
spheres mandated their retreat into the home from the
workshop or counter of their husbands' business. Carriages
and chaperones both protected them from the danger of the

streets and displayed their status – a status heavily reliant on their sexual purity as a guarantee of property and inheritance.[2] As chivalry became an increasingly important component of manliness, middle-class men were told to control their own passions and protect ladies from those men who lacked such control.

Reformers also wished to control the unruly working-class culture of the streets and protect the middle class from the criminal elements which supposedly lurked there. This protection, however, led to regulation of those women, especially prostitutes, who resisted such restrictions and claimed the freedom of the streets.

Working-class women continued to traverse the streets and fields of England out of necessity. A.J. Munby noted their presence on London Bridge:

> London Bridge, more than any place I know here, seems to be the great thoroughfare for young women and girls. One meets them at every step: young women carrying large bundles of umbrella-frames home to be covered; young women carrying wooden cages full of hats, which yet want the silk and binding; costergirls, often dirty and sordid, going to fill their empty baskets, and above all, female sackmakers.[3]

Even servant girls had to go out on dark, rainy nights for errands, or walk long miles in search of home or another place. As their amusements took place away from the parental roof, at work, in pubs, or in pleasure-gardens, working women enjoyed both sexual freedom – and risks.

Their freedom violated middle-class notions of propriety. Ignoring the importance of working women in the British economy, moralists wished to limit their movements to the domestic sphere. As we have seen, judges and doctors used their authority in the courtroom to impose bourgeois standards on working-class women, and legislation such as the New Poor Law enshrined their power.

The explosion of the popular press after 1800 enabled their moral pronouncements to reach far beyond the courtroom. When one judge told a convicted rapist, 'The treatment which the girl has received from you, will be a warning to others, not to enter into that familiarity and form an acquaintance with persons so unknown to them as it appears you were to her',[4] he addressed a national audience. By the 1820s newspapers – including the respectable *Times* – relied on extensive criminal court reporting to enliven their otherwise dull menu of Parliamentary debates. Their vague, moralistic descriptions of assaults as 'too disgusting to relate' rendered rape all the more frightening: it became a nameless, shadowy horror, an assault on women's moral integrity rather than on her person. Newspapers suppressed women's own accounts of rape as indecent: in their place they substituted the lesson of rape as a warning to women to behave. The controversy over Mary Ashford's death enabled such warnings to reach far beyond journalism to pervade English popular culture. Local and London newspapers reported Thornton's trial, and this sensational case also furnished the plots for at least three melodramas (one performed as late as 1871) and lurid pamphlets which were sold on London streets for decades after 1817.[5]

Established bourgeois morality, however, did not entirely dominate this burgeoning popular culture. By the 1830s, radicals began publishing their own illegal newspapers, relying heavily on reports of sex and violence to illustrate aristocratic decadence. They challenged, to some extent, the use of rape as a warning to conform to middle-class standards by defending the freedom of working-class women; but they did so by promulgating their own myth about sexual exploitation. The image of the virtuous village maiden, seduced and abandoned by a wealthy libertine, at once symbolized class exploitation and denied the reality of rape. Working women faced most danger from sexual violence inflicted by men of their own class. And by defending poor women's chastity against imputations of Evangelical moralists, radicals contributed to sexual repression, for in portraying them as passive victims of male lust, they denied women's right to sexual pleasure. Nevertheless, the radical press did counter established middle-class morality. It ensured that the eventual triumph of Victorian ideals of feminine behaviour was the outcome of prolonged negotiations within popular culture rather than the unresisted imposition of middle-class morality.

Mary Ashford

The controversy over Mary Ashford's death can be taken to mark the beginning of these negotiations, for the scandal aroused by Thornton's acquittal led to intense public scrutiny of women's freedom in plebeian culture. Mary Ashford was a servant girl from Erdington, a rural village near Birmingham. On 26 May 1817 she decided to amuse herself by attending a country dance in a nearby pub. There she met bricklayer Abraham Thornton; by midnight, they left to wander the dark fields together. Mary Ashford was last seen sitting on a stile with Thornton at four o'clock in the morning; only an hour later, neighbours pulled her bruised and lacerated body from a shallow pond.

Thornton's acquittal for her rape and murder by a local jury of tradesmen and farmers sparked popular outrage. Polemicists conducted a pamphlet war over Thornton's guilt, local ballads celebrated Mary Ashford's virtue, and playwrights embellished this rural crime into a plot for Birmingham and London stages.

It is possible that local people maligned Thornton so virulently because he endangered the trust between men and women necessary for the sexual freedom of plebeian courtship mores. Before the rape and murder, both Ashford's and Thornton's behaviour was quite unremarkable; Mary Ashford merely followed local custom by 'walking out' with a young man she did not know very well. One witness in the trial had seen the couple on a stile at three o'clock in the morning because he had just come from courting his sweetheart in the parlour while her farmer father slept upstairs.[6] A later court case from the Birmingham area, an action for seduction, revealed that no one in Mary Turner's family rebuked her when she courted several different men, walking in the fields during summer evenings, or found it unusual when she spent the night in a pub with her fiancé after he bought their wedding ring.[7]

A defence of rural mores, however, never entered the controversy, for the melodramatic versions of the murder concealed the very normality of Mary Ashford's conduct. Melodrama transformed this bricklayer into the son of a gentleman who bribed the jury to ensure his acquittal, linking him with the villainous aristocratic libertine of myth. In the play *The Murdered Maid*, 'Maria' cries to 'Thornville' as he chases her, 'Begone, and learn that the humble and lowborn Maria abhors the wretch, though a diadem sparkled on his brows, who would shock her ears with such base proposals, and try to lure her from the paths of rectitude and honour.'[8]

Even when they did not distort Thornton's class origins, polemicists portrayed him as 'unnatural', 'mad', a monstrous beast completely different from normal men. As her staunch defender the Rev. Luke Booker thundered, 'Mary Ashford was savagely seized by a Sabine, and after experiencing the most brutal treatment, inhumanly immolated by her rapacious defiler!'[9]

By elevating Mary Ashford's murder into myth, these melodramatic depictions ultimately reinforced patriarchal assumptions and concealed the reality of male violence. The portrayal of Thornton as an aristocratic libertine or monster implied that women need only fear mad strangers of a different class. In fact, as we have seen, sexual violence was not uncommon in plebeian courtship in the early nineteenth century.

Middle-class observers seized the opportunity to criticize this courtship pattern and impose restrictions on female behaviour. Thornton's defenders maintained that Mary Ashford's 'imprudent' actions excused his admitted violence, which they defined as normal masculine 'persuasion'. Edward Holroyd dismissed the evidence of bruises on Ashford's arms and lacerations on her genitals by arguing,

> There were no appearances but what might have been from a connection obtained by consent after considerable earnestness, exertion, and importunity . . . the deceased,

after some efforts to get away, and struggle and resistance at first, yielded, a yielding obtained most probably reluctantly, and by artifice, promises, and oaths, and urgent importunity, to which her own extreme imprudence in remaining alone with a man, especially one so shortly known to her, all night in the fields, she was unfortunately exposed.[10]

Holroyd's acceptance of violence as a technique of seduction was not unusual; as we have seen, men often claimed that women 'consented' to violence, and doctors justified these claims. Thornton's defenders smugly implied it was women's responsibility to defend themselves against uncontrollable male passion – if they failed, the taint of immorality was their own. Holroyd and others surmised that Mary Ashford drowned herself out of shame at yielding to Thornton.

Others violently disagreed: Thornton had violated the ideals of chivalrous manhood as well as Mary Ashford's virginity. The melodramas about the murder warned, 'Oh giddy youth beware;/May virtue, sense, and honour, hold control,/Ere furious passions stain the spotless soul.'[11] One attorney characterized Holroyd's claims as 'licentious sentiments' which were 'an atrocious libel on the whole female race'.[12] Mary Ashford's popularity as a heroine overwhelmed Thornton's defenders. She inspired both local ballads reviling Thornton and an adulatory article in the genteel pages of the *Ladies Monthly Magazine*. This journal portrayed her as the archetypal seduced maiden of romance:

She promised, at a very early age, to rise superior to her station by the graces of her mind and person . . . so lovely a girl could not have been without admirers, but it was proved, that although she had a great share of vivacity, it was so tempered by discretion, that scandal itself could not cast aspersion on her fair fame . . . she was of a retired and domestic turn.[13]

Although no other evidence confirms this docile portrait, its unquestioning support for Mary Ashford represents female sympathy for the victim of male violence, albeit a sympathy bound by bourgeois domesticity.

The controversy strengthened middle-class values of chastity rather than defending older community mores. Popular literature, influenced by middle-class norms, depicted Mary Ashford as valuing her chastity above her life – a doubtful assumption given the acceptance of premarital sex in her community. In one melodrama, Thornville remembers Maria crying, 'Oh reflect, if once a female falls from virtue, abandoned by all, she exceeds man in the extent of wickedness.'[14]

Even Mary Ashford's chivalrous defenders turned her fate into a warning, unrealistically attempting to restrict the labour and amusements of young working women to the patriarchal household. Although Mary Ashford attended the dance with her 'intimate friend' Hannah Cox, the Reverend Booker stressed her 'imprudence' in frequenting a dance 'unattended by a discreet Male Relative, or a prudent Matron-Friend'.[15] As one writer sardonically noted of Booker, 'Really, if the doctor went on in this manner, his cookmaid will not be able to cross the street with a pie to the baker's without a chaperone.'[16] Yet even commercial ballad publishers, presumably responsive to working-class culture, spread such warnings to young women. 'Mary Ashford's Tragedy', a Birmingham song, celebrates her innocence, but it ends with the requisite moral note:

> Now all you young virgins that bloom'd as I bloom'd,
> Keep at home in your proper employ;
> Ne'er in dancing delight,
> Nor be out at night,
> Nor in the fields roam,
> With a stranger from home,
> Lest you meet a fate as wretched as I.[17]

Women and the freedom of London streets

Attempts to terrorize women into staying in their proper place became more and more common after Mary Ashford's death. Newspapers began to publicize the frequent indecent assaults on respectable women in London streets as a reason to restrict women's freedom: as a police court reporter wrote in 1823, such attacks rendered it 'absolutely dangerous for a decent female to be out by herself after nightfall'.[18] These warnings derived more from increasingly strict definitions of decency than from the increasing incidence of assault.

As we have seen in Chapter 2, indecent assaults and rapes did occur on London streets in the eighteenth century, but the fear of sexual violence was rarely used to keep women out of public space. Even the attacks in 1791 of Renwick Williams, a man known as 'The Monster' who earned that epithet by following ladies down dark streets, cursing and wounding them, failed to terrorize them into domestic confinement. After his trial in 1791, a satirical letter implored the *Diary* newspaper to lay to rest the rumour that a group of 'Men-Monsters' were wounding women in the streets, alleging that it had been propagated by a group of husbands 'to more effectively keep their wives at home'. The plan had backfired, stated the petitioners: 'The said report has already been productive of much evil in domestic pouting, ill-humour, and other consequences of staying at home, contrary to one's will and inclination.' They wished to 'again enjoy those hours of ease, comfort, and quiet, which they experienced in the absence of their wives . . .'[19]

By the 1820s, however, the notion that sexual violence made the streets unsafe for respectable women was rarely questioned; it reinforced the burgeoning ideology of separate spheres, which defined public space as male and the domestic sphere as female. Staid tea-parties, church-going, or at most rounds of calls replaced the attendance at skittles grounds, pleasure gardens, theatres, and masquerades of the wealthy eighteenth-century woman. The appearance of newspaper reports about sexual violence that warned 'decent females' to stay home must therefore be understood in the larger context of women's move into this newly defined private space. Travelling alone was defined by moralists as improper; the fear of rape made it seem dangerous too.

The notion that 'decent' women would be afraid to venture

unprotected out of doors, of course, called into question the decency of those women who were assaulted. Husbands or fathers were expected to be present or even to speak for their wives and daughters when they came before a magistrate; conversely, their absence shed suspicion on a woman's charge. When a Mrs Cullum claimed she had been assaulted in a railway car, the company's barrister pointed out that Richard Kim, her defender, lived at her address but was not her husband. He declared it would have been more 'seemly and proper' for her husband to provide such advocacy.[20]

Men who were publicly accused of molesting women often claimed their victims were not decent or respectable, but the definition of decency was open to debate during this period. In 1825, two ladies accused barrister George Price of indecent exposure in Maiden Lane; apparently, he had been urinating in the street, behaviour no longer acceptable after the introduction of street lamps. He countered that 'the females were not ladies of extreme delicacy, seeing that they went home unprotected by any male companion at so late an hour as 12 o'clock at night.' Bow Street magistrate Mr Minshull defended them against these insinuations, declaring, 'Still they may be respectable; they might have come from the theatre, or the house of a friend in the neighbourhood.'[21].

The imposition of the middle-class standards of separate spheres was a long, protracted process which was much resisted. Many women of the lower-middle class continued to walk to work or to visit at night and still regarded themselves as respectable. When a newspaper report described a victim of indecent assault as a 'respectable married women' or 'decent female' it is difficult to discern her class status. Reporters described wives of surgeons and tradesmen, servants, and laundresses as 'respectable'.[22]

The myth of rape as warning, however, also had implications for the respectable status of men: it was based on the premise of chivalry, that good men would protect their women from bad men. Chivalrous manliness became increasingly important during this period as the middle class defined itself as morally superior to the decadent aristocracy – and of course also asserted its claims to political power. By blaming the frequent indecent assaults on the streets on 'fashionable young men', newspapers criticized gentlemen for not upholding this ideal of manliness. One account refers to an assault by 'two gentlemen of fashion', comparing them to the aristocrats Waldegrave and Waterford who were prosecuted for a similar attack. Deploring the token amounts these molesters were fined, the *Weekly Dispatch* rhetorically queried,

> What is the conclusion? That any of the Waterfordists, or Waldegravites, may seize any poor man's, tradesmen's, or respectable gentlemen's wife, sister, or daughter round the waist in the open streets, throw her on the ground in a violent manner, fall upon her, ruin her bonnet and her parasol, may knock down her companion, whether it be her husband, brother, friend, or lover, brutally beat him as he lies senseless, all for the paltry price of a few pounds. The bosom swells with disgust and indignation at such a decision.[23]

According to Walter of *My Secret Life*, middle-class men had no compunctions about accosting single working women on the street.[24] But working-class men took similar freedoms; in fact, the 'fashionable young men' who so offended the *Weekly Dispatch* turned out to be carpenters. Not only aristocratic libertines, but men of all classes endangered women's freedom.

The ostensible protection of women masked not only restrictions on their activities but the extent of real violence. Men could take advantage of women's fear and turn chivalrous overtures into assault. Eighteen-year-old Elizabeth Hartman, a sailor's wife, spent the evening in a Pentonville pub with three men who promised to accompany her home to Clerkenwell, vowing that 'as they were married men themselves, they could take proper care of her.' Their 'care' involved gagging and gang-raping her in a nearby field.[25] In another instance, Mrs Elizabeth Barlow, the wife of an unemployed dyer, stopped at an alehouse to rest on a journey for her husband's business. She asked two other customers for directions, but instead of leading her to Poplar as they promised her, they raped her.[26]

By the 1820s, chivalry was not enough to shield respectable Londoners from the 'criminal classes', as the poor were characterized; a professional corps of law enforcers seemed to be necessary. The appearance of warnings to women about the danger of the streets must therefore be put in the specific context of the agitation for the New Police as well as the long-term development of separate spheres. As early as 1785 at least one woman felt a police force would allow women to traverse London streets safely; she wrote to *The Times* under the name of 'Andromache' protesting that no one had rescued her from a brutal assault.[27] But the fear of a despotic standing army or secret police force, as was thought to exist in Paris, deterred the establishment of a professional constabulary. During the early nineteenth century, however, especially after the Napoleonic Wars, middle-class Londoners became increasingly concerned with the danger and disorder of the streets, fearing radical agitation as well as criminal activity. The population of London grew over 21 per cent between 1811 and 1821; whereas the poor and the more prosperous lived in the same neighbourhoods in the eighteenth century, distinguished by the grandeur or squalor of their dwellings, by the early nineteenth century bourgeois Londoners began to move south and west, segregating themselves into suburbs and exclusive areas such as Belgravia.[28] The New Police was seen to be necessary as a proxy for middle-class control of the distant, potentially dangerous, poor.

Improved local government began the slow process of sanitary reform and street lighting, while Parliament finally overcame its distrust of governmental forces of order and approved the New Police in 1828. Publicity about attacks on 'respectable women' no doubt contributed to these reforms.

In order to inculcate habits of wage-labour and industrial discipline into the masses of the working poor, the reformers who had been advocating the establishment of a professional force wished to separate out the 'rough' and the 'respectable'. This task gained impetus after the end of the Napoleonic Wars caused an economic depression, increasing the numbers of the poor on London's streets; this same period saw an intensified concern with the problem of prostitution.[29] The philosophy behind the New Police, first articulated in 1800 by magistrate Patrick Colquehoun, was one of 'unremitting vigilance' over working-class culture, in order to hasten and regulate the process of proletarianization: Colquehoun abhorred the way many of the poor made their living scavenging bits of rags, bones, metal scraps, dung, anything imaginable, in fact, which would then be recycled for tiny profits; he believed such activities often merged into theft.[30]

The bawdy songs of ballad mongers and the coarse cries of costermongers, not to mention the 'indecent behaviour' of streetwalkers, embarrassed middle-class men and women and distracted trade from their more established, capitalized shops. One tradesman on the Commercial Road in the East End protested that 'respectable females could not go out of doors without being insulted or shocked beyond description by the indecent conduct and disgusting language of the unfortunate wretches who congregated there.'[31] Interestingly enough, Colquehoun believed that respectable women would find these scenes of vice so alluring that they would surrender their virtue.[32] In any case, advocates of the New Police accused the old style constables of refusing to help women who were assaulted on the streets, but also of being so involved in prostitution themselves that they exacerbated, rather than ameliorated, the danger of the streets.[33]

'Andromache' could never have predicted that the police force she so ardently advocated would have restricted women's freedoms still more. In their zeal to clean up public space, the New Police regarded any woman on the streets at night as a potential streetwalker rather than the object of protective care. Characterizations of prostitutes as 'nymphs of the pave' or less poetically, 'women of the streets', undermined the respectability of any woman walking alone or with a man. Assailants often attempted to excuse their violence by claiming that complainants had tried to extort money, annoyed them, or simply that they were loose women. William Munro, 'a young man of fashionable exterior', swore he struck and wounded Mary Birkett because he thought she was a prostitute, although in fact she was a 'respectable married woman of Hoxton, who had been walking with her husband at midnight down City Road.'[34] Another man whom *The Times* described as 'having the exterior appearance of a gentleman' was charged by a 'respectable married female' named Mary Prescott with indecently assaulting her and throwing her to the ground, and also harassing her female friend with three other 'gentlemen'. He claimed, 'the females coquetted with them, and they were induced to believe they were women of the town.'[35]

The efforts of constables to 'forbid women to walk the streets in a peaceable manner' added to the *Weekly Dispatch*'s campaign against the New Police. In fact, the New Police excited general outrage in radical newspapers and among working people for their repression of working-class street culture and political meetings, outrage which in 1833 and 1848 burst into riots. Referring to an inspector notorious for his 'methodistical' harassment of poor women, the *Weekly Dispatch* queried, 'Can it be true that he took into custody two girls who were returning from the theatre with their parents, and told them they had no business to be out after 12 o'clock at night?'[36]

The Police not only limited the freedom of all women to freely walk the streets; they, like the non-uniformed young men who found amusement in indecent assault, molested women themselves. The *Weekly Dispatch* reported several instances of policemen who raped or indecently assaulted young women and girls. In 1837, it noted that as Charlotte Avis, a ten-year-old girl, walked through Kennington, a policeman named Dowding promised to show her the way but then proceeded to molest her.[37] In 1844 P.C. Weaver escaped a charge of raping Constantina Jones in a public thoroughfare because she lived in a brothel.[38]

However, prostitutes, working-class women, and lower-middle-class matrons all objected to these restrictions on their freedom of movement, for their version of respectable womanhood differed from the helpless femininity of separate spheres. Not only did they continue to walk about the streets and bring their assailants before magistrates, they fought off their attackers when they could. In 1843 a serjeant called Mrs Eliza Badman a prostitute as she came home from the theatre through Shoreditch with her husband and friends. Enraged, 'this respectably dressed . . . wife of a licensed victualler' assaulted him.[39] 'Respectable married women' often collared the drunken young men who insulted them, or indignantly beat them with their umbrellas.[40] When publican Edward Thomas of Grosvenor Mews molested his neighbour Mrs Renwick, 'he got so roughly handled by that lady, as to be obliged to keep to his bed for several weeks.'[41]

However, notions of respectability and modesty limited these women's protests to individual incidents. As Lambeth magistrate Mr Coombe noted, 'the more decent or respectable females were, the more reluctant they were in coming forward to give public details of such gross outrages.'[42] Only prostitutes, who had no respectability to lose, could effectively retaliate against the police: one streetwalker known as 'Lady Barrymore', a violent alcoholic, terrorized beadles, watchmen and police constables for years.[43] In 1840, prostitutes of Waterloo Road used rough music and hot pokers to resist attempts by the policemen and 'respectable inhabitants' to suppress their trade. Ironically, the motive for suppressing their trade was that 'respectable women' could not pass along the street.[44] Was it really the annoyance of prostitutes which kept ladies off the street; or did men drive ladies out by harassing any woman on Waterloo Road as a prostitute?

Ann Crotchley

While the radical press reported such incidents with delight and exposed every possible oppression of prostitutes by the police, it had always been more concerned with portraying women of the streets as passive victims of upper-class lust than with defending the aggressive freedom of plebeian females. A controversy over the rape-murder of Ann Crotchley in Oxford in 1827 reveals the limitations of this sympathy. No matter how far her fall could be attributed to aristocratic decadence, or how vigorously she resisted the police, the image of the degraded prostitute served as the most horrific warning to women to retain their chastity as all costs.

In December 1827, Ann Crotchley bled to death from two wounds in her vagina, inflicted on her while she lay unconscious from intoxication in an Oxford alley. She did not attain Mary Ashford's celebrated status; instead, her murder served as a grisly reminder of the fate of unchaste women. But the progression of newspaper reports about her death reveals a more complex discourse, demonstrating the tension between a popular tendency to sympathize with fallen women and the moralistic desire to attribute their sufferings to sin. Her fate incited a furore in Oxford and London newspapers lasting for several weeks. Although circumstantial evidence pointed to a painter named John Williams as her murderer, the newspapers never reported if he was brought to trial or the case dismissed.

The Times and the *Sun* (a less illustrious London daily) first reported the murder in almost exactly the same words. With melodramatic rhetoric, they depicted Ann Crotchley as a seduced maiden dragged into prostitution by aristocratic vice:

> The unfortunate young woman who has been so inhumanly murdered was about 23 years of age, and of great personal beauty . . . she was a native of Herefordshire, and her family are in a respectable station of life in that part. She had not been many months in the city, whither she was brought by a young gentleman who seduced her away from the parental roof, and then abandoned her to the world. Thus situated, without a friend to her, she became a prey to prostitution, but was remarkable for the mildness of her manners; and she was far beyond the class of such unfortunate outcasts, that her fate appeared to excite great commiseration.[45]

In the same report, however, *The Times* had already begun to demolish Crotchley's status as victim, omitting the *Sun*'s statement, 'There could be no doubt but she had been violated.' Presumably the more established journal considered that a prostitute could not be raped.

A few days later, newspapers ceased to draw on the myth of

the seduced maiden and began to revile Crotchley according to the harsh tenets of Evangelicalism and Utilitarianism, in which prostitutes were hated and feared as the criminal dregs of society. Ann Crotchley's mother, a Hereford glovemaker, revealed in an interview that the supposed 'young gentleman' was in fact a 'notorious pickpocket' incarcerated in Reading Gaol. A 'habitual drunkard and altogether uneducated', Ann Crotchley began prostituting herself in Hereford and only interrupted her career with a stint in the London penitentiary for fallen women.[46]

Despite this scornful depiction of her life, civilized sensibilities could not accept the brutality of her death. Her unnatural wounds precluded the explanation that she was, like Mary Ashford, the victim of overenthusiastic seduction. An Oxford newspaper, reflecting on the 'improbability that any such monster could be found capable of wilfully inflicting such a wound', attributed her death to an accident caused by excessive drinking and even speculated that she had mutilated herself.[47]

To refute this persistent allegation, the coroner exhumed her body and once again asserted that Ann Crotchley was murdered. His evidence was grim but clinical:

> I found the linen saturated with blood . . . . On the left breast and arm, and on the thigh and breast, were recent and severe bruises. I was immediately struck by the sight of two incised wounds inflicted laterally into this cavity . . . . The wound was not clean cut, but appeared to have been inflicted with some force.[48]

Later *The Times* lifted its * * * and described the 'cavity' as 'the passage called the vagina, leading to the mouth of the womb.'[49] Reporters could only use such explicit language – extremely rare in contemporary newspapers – because as a prostitute, Ann Crotchley's body was considered public property. The medical terminology depersonalized the murder, transforming it into a bizarre horror rather than an individual tragedy, and confronting the reader with the very corporeality which degraded Ann Crotchley as a fallen woman.

It is not surprising that public opinion ultimately blamed women for the murder. On 31 December *The Times* suggested that the authorities take note of another case:

> The sufferer, too, was of the same unhappy class, and her destroyers were rival women of the town who had been exasperated by the success of her superior attractions. The modes of vengeance in these cases are not those which occur to a man, however fiendishly malignant or wantonly savage he might be.[50]

The juxtaposition of the 17 December story about her questionable past with a report of seduction underlined the message of Ann Crotchley's death. Chivalry would only uphold the honour of those women who stayed within their place; public violence threatened those who would not conform to the feminine role. If sentimental tales did not get the message across, her brutal murder would.

Conclusion

The increased publicity about sexual assault in the early nineteenth century ostensibly derived from a moral concern with the protection of women, but, like the legal reforms of the same era, it in fact served to regulate and restrict the boundaries of proper feminine behaviour.

The boundaries, however, were the subject of intense negotiation. While the middle-class ideology of separate spheres would confine women to the home, lower-middle-class women claimed their right to venture abroad on business or pleasure without losing their respectability. Radicals recognized that the efforts of the New Police to suppress prostitution would also infringe working-class women's necessary freedom to traverse London's streets. They defended victims of sexual violence, such as Mary Ashford, by portraying them as casualties of upper-class exploitation.

Yet the heroic status accorded to women who proved that rape was a fate worse than death by suffering murder merely upheld the patriarchal valuation of chastity. Ann Crotchley's fate reveals how quickly sentimental rhetoric evaporated when confronted with the brutality of real violence and women who flaunted their defiance of patriarchal, bourgeois control.

And melodramatic transformation of the mundane status of most rapists into glamorous villains could not conceal the fact that chivalry was the biggest protection racket ever invented. The danger of sexual assault in the public places was real, for sexually harassing women continued to be a popular amusement for men of all classes. However, the myth of rape as warning implied that women would be safe in the domestic sphere, protected by patriarchal men. As we have seen, this was a bitter fallacy.

CHAPTER 8

Conclusion: patriarchal myths, feminist challenges

Rape trials provided titillating reading for eighteenth-century gentlemen, but by the early nineteenth century chivalry supplanted libertinism as the dominant masculine ethos. Chivalrous concern, however, focused on the preservation of female virtue rather than the defence of women's integrity: protection had its price. Legal reforms both eased prosecution for rape and intensified regulation of working women's sexuality. Charities aided 'fallen women' – if they repented of their sins. Newspapers thundered against fashionable young men who indecently assaulted London ladies – and advised all respectable women to keep off the streets. Proletarian radicals blamed aristocratic libertines for seducing poor village maidens, but their mythic rhetoric concealed the reality of sexual violence within the working class.

The dichotomy of chastity and unchastity structured these discourses, defining rape not as the violation of a woman's body but as the theft of her virtue. Three major consequences stemmed from these discourses. First, they robbed women of their ability to articulate their own experiences of rape, and imparted a sense of shame to women who felt they had lost their honour. Second, these discourses magnified a thousand-fold individual men's power to terrify women through rape, for fear served to warn women to behave according to restrictive middle-class standards. Third, they concealed the reality of violence against women. No matter how a woman behaved, men – lovers, masters, fathers, strangers, neighbours – could rape her with near impunity.

While most men did not rape, the roots of sexual violence lay not in social or individual pathology but in the 'normal' structures of patriarchal society. Because female sexuality was regarded as a 'commodity' a man could sometimes believe he had a right to 'take' his fiancée whether she consented or not; despotic fathers who regarded their children as their property could occasionally excuse their sexual abuse. Violence thus entered courtship and fatherhood, supposed sanctums of love. In both the eighteenth and nineteenth centuries, female servants were raped by their masters, but apprentices also sometimes raped their masters' daughters, and fellow servants were perhaps the most dangerous men of all. Libertinism was a continuous, though sometimes underground, current in masculine and elite culture, as expressed in gang rape, indecent assaults on London streets, and pornography.

Despite the suppression of their speech and the terror of sexual violence, some women did manage to fight back. Brave women defied judges' scorn in the Old Bailey. Some petitioners to the charitable institution asserted they were victims of force, not their own sin, even if officials rarely heard them. London matrons ignored magistrates' warnings and continued to attend the theatre, fending off their attackers with umbrellas. Hannah Cullwick, Victorian maid-servant, walked through London's dark streets at night, safe in the knowledge that her 13" biceps enabled her to defend herself against obnoxious young gentlemen. Female readers celebrated Mary Ashford as a heroine, not as an example of imprudence. Their much criticized immodesty enabled factory girls to defend each other against gang rape, while servants rebuked masters for fondling them and threatened those who persisted. Prostitutes continued to ply their trade on darkened streets and took violent revenge against the men who overstepped the boundaries of sexual transactions.

Popular culture also provided exemplars of resistance, albeit ones which portrayed rape as a fate worse than death. In song, the milkmaid thrust a rapier into the lascivious squire, who rewarded her valour with riches. Emily Fitzor-mond, heroine of a penny-issue novel of that name, was rescued from two fashionable officers by her friend Patty, who 'snatched a couple of pistols from the mantlepiece . . . completely astonishing them with the boldness of her conduct.'[1] By the late 1830s and 1840s, however, the simple theme of virtue rewarded for bold resistance faded in favour of the fragile romantic heroine. The cheapest Sunday newspapers still occasionally featured heroines who cried 'Unhand me, villain!' and plunged a stiletto into a libertine's heart. But they were overshadowed by frail maidens who required rescue by manly yeomen, and victims of rape who chose death over dishonour. While radical fiction attributed women's fall to poverty and injustice, its seduced heroines almost always died in implicit atonement for their shame.[2]

Women could not publicly protest rape, for they were forbidden to speak about sex at all. Those who did, such as Mary Wollstonecraft and the Owenite socialist-feminists, were reviled as unnatural and immodest. Middle-class women did organize around the issue of prostitution as early as the 1830s, portraying fallen women as victims of entrapment and violation, but they subsumed their activities under male control and masculine rhetoric. The Associate Institute for Improving and Enforcing the Laws for the Protection of Women refused to press Parliament for punishment of seducers, claiming that 'the unhappy victims' must avoid public shame and forgive their violators.[3] The Female Penitentiary defined young prostitutes, unmarried mothers, common-law wives, and rape victims alike as fallen women who must atone for their sins.[4]

Today the word chastity is not often heard; Victorian prudishness seems outmoded and irrelevant. We are no longer imprisoned in a sexual economy in which our chastity is our most valuable possession; although women still earn much less than men, most women can afford to regard sexuality as a source of pleasure, not profit. But how much has changed in terms of sexual violence since the early nineteenth century? The continued prevalence of rape by friends, acquaintances, and husbands as well as strangers; sexual harassment by employers and co-workers, and attacks on lesbians who live openly, indicate that not all men acknowledge our right to desire or refuse.

The myth of rape as a warning to women continues to haunt us. As the women of the London Rape Crisis Centre have written, 'We live in this society as though we were in a state of siege, and what's more, we are made to feel as though we are responsible for it.'[5] Authorities publicize every spectacular rape in a way which perpetually reinforces the notion that to be safe women must be sheltered at home, or only go out accompanied by a man. Judges still blame women for making themselves vulnerable to rape by taking ordinary freedoms, and the gruelling cross-examinations women face in court continue to categorize them as chaste or unchaste. In 1982, Judge Bertrand Richards stated, 'It is the height of imprudence for any girl to hitchhike alone at night . . . she is in the true sense asking for it.'[6] When Peter Sutcliffe terrorized Yorkshire women, police authorities augmented the terror by warning all women not to venture outdoors in the evening. Police and journalists reacted with horror only when Sutcliffe began to murder 'innocent' women, as if his attacks on prostitutes merely punished them for their 'guilty' behaviour.[7] The denigration of victims' virtue also enables judges to excuse rapists' crimes: only 34 per cent of all men reported to the police are ever convicted, a figure little changed from the early nineteenth century.[8] Judge Richards refused to imprison the man who raped a woman who was hitchhiking, merely fining him £2,000.[9]

Discourses about rape, however, have changed in two major, but contradictory ways: the myth of female masochism has further eroded women's credibility, while feminists now assert our own definition of rape. In her book *Female Sexuality and the Law*, Susan Edwards has demonstrated how in the late nineteenth century, medical experts and the gutter press together 'helped create and maintain a belief in the lying, imagining, hysterical, and malicious rape complainant.'[10] The British police continue to treat rape victims according to such stereotypes: in 1984, a London police chief wrote an article in his local newspaper which alleged 'that all women who report rape to the police are either lying, mad, or having sexual fantasies.'[11] Until recently many 'experts' testified in court that it was not possible to rape a healthy, adult woman, implying that if a woman claimed she was raped, she really wanted it.

After 1900 psychoanalysis added a new twist to the image of the hysterical rape victim – this was the theory of feminine masochism. Its popularizers, such as Helene Deutsch, proclaimed that women not only enjoy violent sex but actively precipitate it, thus 'scientifically' validating claims rapists have made since the early nineteenth century that women consent to violence. Furthermore, as Edwards has noted, the theory of the subconscious mind coupled with the notion of feminine masochism reinforced allegations that women who accused men of rape actually fantasized the assaults. Lord Hailsham enshrined these insinuations into law in the 1975 case Rex *v.* Morgan, in which three men raped a woman after her husband told them that when she said no she really wanted to be forced. He reduced their sentences on the grounds that they genuinely believed she consented.[12]

The psychoanalytic exploration of childhood sexuality has also reinforced the notion that children lie about sexual assault. Freud's repression of his own discovery that many middle-class Viennese women had been 'seduced' by their fathers formed the basis of his insights into the unconscious mind and the Oedipal complex, but it also had pernicious consequences for the treatment of incest survivors. As Judith Herman writes, 'The legacy of Freud's inquiry into the subject of incest, still shared by professionals and laymen alike, is that children lie about sexual abuse.'[13] Psychiatry often defines young victims as seductive and perpetrators as sick men who must be pitied, which may explain why the rape of female children is now much less severely punished than in the nineteenth century. In the North-east between 1800 and 1829, 80 per cent of men accused of rape or attempted rape on young girls were punished by imprisonment, or more rarely, hanging. In 1980, however, out of 254 men reported to the British police for the rape of young girls, only fifty-four were cautioned and forty-five sentenced to immediate imprisonment after trial.[14] These criticisms are not meant to invalidate the insights of psychoanalysis, but to point out how patriarchal interests can infect ostensibly scientific discourses.

Feminists, however, have broken the silence about rape, challenging masculine discourses with our own definitions. But it has been a long, slow process to enable women's voices to be heard. By the 1860s, as Judith Walkowitz has written, feminists proclaimed their own discourses about prostitution in the struggle against the Contagious Diseases Act. This legislation attempted to prevent venereal disease by forcing suspected prostitutes in garrison towns to submit to medical examinations and registration, outraging both middle-class women and working-class men who protested against the indignities of 'instrumental rape' and the public humiliation of poor women. Feminists who campaigned against the Acts asserted their right as women to organize autonomously and speak out on sexual matters, repudiating the conventional division of women into respectable and fallen.[15]

It was difficult for women to sustain publicly such a daring position. A few years later, as Walkowitz has recently written, feminists' protests about Jack the Ripper were barely heard, as doctors and detectives again swamped public consciousness with their expert discourses about the murderer as a madman, and working men threatened to 'rip' their wives.[16] The 'white slavery' scandal, about the abduction and violation of thirteen-year-old girls into prostitution, outraged feminists but also led to the repression of working-class girls' freedom. While contemporary historians often analyse the hysteria over the aristocratic exploitation of female children as the result of middle-class anxiety about childhood sexuality, it must be remembered that this may also have reflected the deep-rooted popular hatred of child molesters.

Advocates of social purity seized centre stage in the late nineteenth-century debates on sexual offences, basing their actions (such as the incarceration of runaway young girls) on chivalrous notions of safeguarding chastity. Nonetheless, the National Vigilance Campaign did provide 'solicitors to conduct prosecutions in innumerable cases of rape and attempted rape, sexual assault or indecent exposure, and took non-judicial action in cases such as . . the sexual harassment of young women in the streets.'[17] Jan Lambertz has revealed that in some late nineteenth- and early twentieth-century mill towns, unions actively mobilized against the sexual harassment, responding to the needs of their female members. The motives of male union officials were mixed: some wished to enforce the purity of the home, or to strengthen their organizations' local hold, but these unions did acknowledge that women had a legitimate place in the mills as wage earners and had the right to work there without sexual harassment.[18]

As Linda Gordon and Ellen Dubois have recently written, nineteenth-century feminists tended to focus on prostitution rather than rape as emblematic of a more general sexual enslavement of women, 'as if the norms of legal sexual intercourse were in themselves so objectionable that rape did not seem that much worse.' But they also regarded prostitutes as passive victims, who were to be protected by wiser middle-class feminists, not as agents who wished to control their own destinies. The other feminist current, they write, ignored sexual danger by celebrating a male-identified sexual pleasure.[19]

Today, the feminist movement has cut through the limitations of moralistic protection and masculine liberation. By defining rape with a dichotomy of desire or refusal, instead of unchastity or chastity, we assert our right to sexual pleasure and our demand to be free from sexual violence. Rape crisis centres enable women to break through the silence of shame; Reclaim the Night marches mark our collective will to traverse city streets without fear, chanting, 'Yes means yes, and no means no, however we're dressed and wherever we go.' Yet we know the fear of rape is real; it is the illusion of safety that is false. Understanding the myth of rape as warning as a historical creation helps us to defy it; defying the reality of sexual violence is a more difficult, but necessary, endeavour.

Class status of assailants and victims in the eighteenth and nineteenth centuries

In order to interpret these tables, we must understand how late eighteenth-century observers understood class status. Contemporary analysts such as the reformer Colquehoun broke down the population into three great sections: the aristocracy, which included fundholders and gentlemen; the middling ranks, encompassing professionals, merchants, clergy, and officers at the upper ranks and tailors, shopkeepers, innkeepers and clerks at the lower; and finally, the 'lower orders', the vast mass of the labouring poor, including artisans, sailors, soldiers, servants, and common labourers.

TABLE 1
Class status of rapists and victims 1770–99, London – Old Bailey sessions

		RAPISTS					
		Upper		Middle		Lower	
		No.	%	No.	%	No.	%
	Upper	0	0	0	0	0	0
VICTIMS	Middle	0	0	5	14	6	17
	Lower	0	0	8	22	17	47

N = 36 when class status of both assailant and victim known

TABLE 2
Class status of rapists and victims 1770–99 from North-east Assize records

| | | RAPISTS | | | | | |
| | | Upper | | Middle | | Lower | |
		No.	%	No.	%	No.	%
	Upper	0	0	0	0	0	0
VICTIMS	Middle	0	0	2	8	6	21
	Lower	1	4	6	21	13	46

N = 28 when class status of both assailant and victim known

TABLE 3
Class status of assailants and victims as compared to population of England in 1806

| | Population[a] of England | London[b] rapists | | London[c] victims | | North-east[d] rapists | | North-east victims | |
	%	No.	%	No.	%	No.	%	No.	%
Class									
Upper	1.4	14	6[e]	0		1	2	0	
Middle	31.6	66	29	13	28	12	24	10	21
Lower	67.0	140	62	27	59	23	48	25	52
Unknown		7	4	6	13	12	25	13	25
	100.0	227	100	46	100	48	100	48	100

[a] from Harold Perkins, *The Origins of Modern English Society*, who derived the percentages from Patrick Colquehoun's figures in his *Treatise in Indigence*, London, 1806.

[b] from Old Bailey Sessions trials for rape and from Middlesex Sessions indictments and recognizances for attempted rape, 1770–5, 1780–5, 1790–5.

[c] from Old Bailey Sessions trials – the Middlesex records do not include class or occupation of victim.

[d] from North-east assize depositions, Public Record Office.

[e] The higher percentage of upper-class assailants is probably due to the fact that in the Middlesex sessions records, many middle-class men preferred to style themselves 'gentlemen'.

TABLE 4
Class of assailant and victim, from Assizes depositions, 1800–29*
(including children)

	Victims (%)	Assailants (%)
Upper-class (gentlemen)	0	3
Middle-class – farmers, shopkeepers, overlookers, masters and their wives and daughters; dressmakers	16	27
Male and female skilled workers, mill workers, and the wives and daughters of the same	16	33
Male and female farm servants, farm labourers, ostlers, soldiers, and the wives and daughters of the same	15	37
Female domestic servants and nurses	53	
Total:	100	100
	N = 55	N = 81

* There is not enough information given in newspaper reports about occupations to construct a similar table.

Relationship of assailant to victim and location of rapes

TABLE 5
Relationship of assailant to victim in the eighteenth century, from Old Bailey and North-east Assize cases

| | London | | North-east | |
	No.	%	No.	%
Strangers	12	27	16	47
Courtship	1	2	1	3
Acquaintance	14	31	12	35
Fellow worker or lodger	8	18	0	0
Master or master's relative	9	20	3	9
Relative of victim – incest	1	2	2	6
	45	100	34	100
Total known to victim	33	73	18	53

Note: No doubt many rapes by masters and other men of higher class were never reported. However, women may have also been reluctant to report rapes by men they knew, such as relatives, fiancés, or friends, as the material from unmarried mothers discussed in Chapter 6 suggests. Women may have been more eager to prosecute masters, in fact, if they perceived rape as thus breaking taboos and taking an unfair advantage of an employment situation. Women were probably most eager to prosecute strangers, but strangers were only apprehended with difficulty. In the assize records of the North-east, strangers comprise 47 per cent of the assailants, but only 27 per cent in the Old Bailey records because these consist of trials, not depositions which could be filed easily enough if the assailant was unknown.

TABLE 6
Location of rapes in the North-east, nineteenth century (not including children)

| | Assize records 1801–29 | | Newspaper accounts 1830–45 | |
	N=	%	N=	%
Travelling				
by a single man	30	38	18	29
gang rape	7	9	15	24
Working outside	13	18	4	6
In the house				
by outside assailant	10	13	9	15
by master, lodger, fellow servant	15	19	12	19
Other	2	3	Factory 4	7
	78	100	62	100
Total while travelling	47%			
Total in the house	32%			

TABLE 7
Relationship of assailant to victim (including children)

| | Assize records 1801–29 | Newspaper accounts 1830–45 |
	%	%
Stranger	26	23
Courtship	5	4
Acquaintance	38	44
Fellow servant or worker	7	8
Master, master's relative or overlooker	20	13
Relative	4	8
	100	100
	N = 76	N = 61

APPENDIX III

Statistics on courtship, proximity and rape in the nineteenth century

TABLE 8
Courtship and rape

Category of father of petitioners' child	Proportion of all fathers		Proportion of all rapists	
	N =	%	N =	%
All courters*	841	81	129	68
(Promise of marriage)	(634)	(61)	(69)	(36)
(No promise)	(212)	(20)	(53)	(28)
Non-courters	199	19	61	32
Total	1040	100	190	100

TABLE 9
Courtship and rape

Category of father of petitioners' child	In each category fathers who were rapists	
	N =	%
All courters*	129	15
(Promise of marriage)	69	11
(No promise)	53	25
Non-courters	61	31
Total	190	

TABLE 10
Courtship, proximity and rape

Category of father of petitioners' child	Proportion of all fathers		Proportion of all rapists	
	N =	%	N =	%
Fellow servants	222	21	59	31
(Courters)*	(187)	(18)	(42)	(22)
(Non-courters)	(33)	(3)	(17)	(9)
Lodgers	137	13	27	14
(Courters)	(114)	(11)	(19)	(10)
(Non-courters)	(23)	(2)	(8)	(4)
Masters	53	5	17	9
Strangers	25	3	11	6
Others (90% are courters)	603	58	76	40
Total	1040	100	190	100
Total proximate fathers	412	39	103	54

TABLE 11
Courtship, proximity and rape

Category of father of petitioners' child	In each category fathers who were rapists	
	N =	%
Fellow servants	59	27
(Courters)*	42	22
(Non-courters)	17	51
Lodgers	27	20
(Courters)	19	17
(Non-courters)	8	35
Masters	17	32
Strangers	11	44
Others (90% courters)	76	13
Total		190
Total proximate fathers	103	25

* Courters include all those men who paid some sort of romantic attention to the petitioner they impregnated.

Source: Foundling Hospital Petitions, 1815–45.

Notes

Chapter 1
Introduction

1 London Rape Crisis Centre, *Sexual Violence: the Reality for Women*, London, the Women's Press, 1984, pp. 129–30; Susan Brownmiller, *Against Our Will: Men, Women, and Rape*, London, Secker & Warburg, 1975, p. 186.

2 Brownmiller, pp. 14–15, 209.

3 Olivia Harris and Kate Young, 'The Subordination of Women in Cross-Cultural Perspective' in *Papers on Patriarchy*, Women's Publishing Collective, Brighton, 1978, p. 40.

4 Michael Foucault, *History of Sexuality*, vol. I, New York, Vintage, 1980; see also critiques in Jeffrey Weeks, *Sex, Politics and Society: The Regulation of Sexuality since 1800*, London, Longman, 1981, p. 7; and Rachel Harrison and Frank Mort, 'Patriarchal aspects of 19th century state formation', in *Capitalism, State Formation and Marxist Theory*, London, Quartet, 1980, pp. 107–8.

5 Susan Edwards, *Female Sexuality and the Law*, Oxford, Martin Robinson, 1981.

6 Leslie Stern, 'Introduction to Plaza', *m/f* No. 4, 1980, p. 24.

7 Angela Davis, *Women, Race and Class*, London, the Women's Press, 1982, Chapter 4. The stereotype of the black rapist was not prevalent in the sources I have examined. The only discussion of a rapist's race that I have found is racist in a different way: appealing for the reprieve of a black man condemned to death for rape, *The Times* noted, 'The criminal is an unenlightened stranger, the native of a country where the indulgence of the passions is legitimate, and where there are no laws, either social, moral or religious to restrain them.' (23 August 1806) There is, however, a fictional portrayal of the rape

143

of a black woman, no doubt drawing on the anti-abolitionist sentiment of the time: in her novel *The Farmer of Inglewood Forest* (London, 1796) Mrs Elizabeth Helme includes the story of a wicked (white) West Indian planter who raped his female slave.

Anti-Irish stereotypes sometimes appear in the reporting of rapes involving Irish people; there seemed to have been a notion that Irish custom allowed a rapist to be forgiven if he married his victim. However, it is possible that this is just an anti-Irish stereotype and I have not gone into the subject because I feel it needs a fuller treatment using Irish sources.

8 Brownmiller, p. 391.

9 Jacques Rossiaud, 'Prostitution, Youth, and Society in the Towns of Southeastern France in the 15th Century' in *Deviants and the Abandoned*, R. Forster and O. Ranum (eds), Baltimore, John Hopkins University Press, 1978, p. 19, and Cissie Fairchilds, 'Female Sexual Attitudes and the Rise of Illegitimacy: A Case Study', *Journal of Interdisciplinary History* vol. 8, Spring 1978, pp. 627–67.

10 Lorenne Clark and Debra J. Lewis, *Rape: the Price of Coercive Sexuality*, Toronto, the Women's Press, 1977, pp. 128–9; Brownmiller, p. 185; Stevi Jackson, 'The social context of rape: sexual scripts and motivation', *Women's Studies International Quarterly*, vol. 1, n. 1 (1978) 27–58.

11 Clark and Lewis pp. 120–1. See also H.C. Barnett, 'The Political Economy of Rape and Prostitution', *Review of Radical Political Economy*, vol. 8, no. 1, 1976, pp. 59–66.

12 Brownmiller, p. 185.

13 For sources for ideas on language, see Terry Lovell, *Pictures of Reality*, London, British Film Institute, 1980, pp. 64–87, and V.N. Volosinov, *Marxism and the Philosophy of Language*, New York, Seminar Press, 1973, p. 85.

14 Catherine MacKinnon, 'Feminism, Marxism, Method, and the State: Toward a Feminist Jurisprudence', *Signs*, vol. 8, no. 4, 1983, p. 648.

15 Catherine MacKinnon, *ibid.*, p. 650. See also Catherine MacKinnon, 'Feminism, Marxism, and the State: an Agenda for Theory', *Signs*, vol. 7, no. 3, 1982, p. 539.

16 Leonore Davidoff and Catherine Hall, 'The Separation of Spheres 1780–1850', Unpublished interim report, University of Essex, 1980, pp. 4, 66.

17 Thomas Laqueur, 'The Queen Caroline Affair', *Journal of Modern History*, vol. 54, September 1982, 417–66.

18 Barbara Taylor, *Eve and the New Jerusalem: Socialism and Feminism in the 19th Century*, New York, Pantheon, 1983, p. 213.

19 Taylor, pp. 193–207.

20 For the Jacobin origins of this image, see Marilyn Butler, *Jane Austen and the War of Ideas*, Oxford, Clarendon Press, 1975, pp. 55–104; also Susan Staves, 'British Seduced Maidens', *Eighteenth Century Studies*, vol. 14, no. 2, Winter 1980/1, pp. 110–15; Martha Vicinus, 'Helpless and Unbefriended: 19th century domestic melodrama', *New Literary History*, vol. 8, no. 1, Autumn 1981, p. 143; and Anna K. Clark, 'The Politics of Seduction in English Popular Culture, 1748–1848', in Jean Radford (ed.), *The Progress of Romance*, History Workshop Series, London, Routledge & Kegan Paul 1986.

21 A.P. Wadsworth, 'Newspaper Circulation 1800–1854', *Transactions of the Manchester Statistical Society*, March 1955, p. 12.

22 R.K. Webb, *The British Working-Class Reader*, London, George Allen & Unwin, 1955, p. 25.

23 Louis James, *Print and the People, 1819–1861*, Harmondsworth, Penguin, 1978; Martha Vicinus, *The Industrial Muse*, London, Croom Helm, 1974; Charles Hindley, *The Life and Times of James Catnach*, Welywn Garden City, Herts., Seven Dials Press, 1970 (1878), pp. 2, 409.

Chapter 2
Women's pain, men's pleasure: rape in the eighteenth century

Note: In this and subsequent chapters I sometimes refer to 'rape victims' or victims of rape. I am aware of the recent movement to avoid such terminology (see London Rape Crisis Centre, *Sexual Violence: the Reality for Women*, London, the Women's Press, 1984, p. 1) and sympathize with its logic: that women's identity should not be defined by their experience of rape. An alternative term is 'survivor'. However, this implies that many women did not survive rape or sexual assault; in my period at least rape-murder was relatively rare, although it did occur. It is simply too cumbersome to write 'women who have been raped', or 'the woman upon whom the assailant inflicted his violence', instead of 'rape victims' or 'his victim'. When I write 'rape victim', however, it should be understood that I do not think that woman's identity was necessarily bound up with her experience of rape: the anger and courage of the women who prosecuted in the Old Bailey trials belies such assumptions. Yet during this period other people often defined rape victims as if the experience did permeate their entire lives: this is an unfortunate historical truth.

1 The involvement of corrupt justices with prostitution was notorious during this period. The anonymous editor of the *Midnight Rambler* (London, 1770, pp. 95, 109), told of watchmen extorting money from prostitutes and brothel-keepers bribing magistrates. Francis Place wrote that the 'trading justices' ordered sweeps of streetwalkers and pocketed their bail money. (Place, Add. Ms. 27, 826ff.142, in British Library Manuscript Department.) William Blackborough, one of these justices, would not allow constables to arrest the thieves or prostitutes who lived in his tenements on crime-ridden Turnmill Street, Clerkenwell, though he was content to harass other streetwalkers (Middlesex Sessions Order Book, September 1790, pp. 77–81, MJ/OC/12, Greater London Record Office).

2 *1811 Dictionary of the Vulgar Tongue*, Adelaide, Australia, Bibliophile Books, London, Macmillan, 1981, (1811).

3 Mary Wollstonecraft in Gary Kelly (ed.), *Mary, a Fiction and the Wrongs of Women*, Oxford University Press, 1976, pp. 103–18. In his introduction Gary Kelly notes that Caroline Blood (sister of Wollstonecraft's beloved friend Fanny), like Jemima, 'is seduced, abandoned, persecuted by the Poor Laws and then forced into prostitution by economic necessity.'

4 Roy Porter, 'Mixed Feelings: the Enlightenment and Sexuality in 18th Century Britain', in Paul-Gabriel Bouce (ed.), *Sexuality in Eighteenth Century Britain*, Manchester University Press, 1982. For libertinism, see issues of *The Rambler's Magazine* of the 1780s, which reported rape in a titillating manner; and the Hellfire and Mohawk clubs of young gentlemen who harassed women in the streets, see Iwan Bloch, *Sexual Life in England*, London, Corgi, 1958, p. 182.

5 *1811 Dictionary of the Vulgar Tongue*.

6 Ivy Pinchbeck, *Women Workers and the Industrial Revolution 1750–1850*, London, Virago, 1981 (1930), p. 56, 163; Pat Hudson, 'Proto-industrialisation: the case of the West Riding textile industry in the 18th and early 19th centuries', *History Workshop Journal*, No. 12, Autumn, 1981, p. 56.

7 Public Record Office, Chancery Lane, North-east Assizes 45/60 Pt. 1, Lent 1827. Hereafter referred to as PRO Assi.

8 PRO Assi. 45/293/188–192, 4 August 1770.

9 For courtship customs, see Rev. J.C. Atkinson, *Forty Years in a Moorland Parish*, London, Macmillan, 1907, p. 5. Also John Gillis, *For Better, For Worse: British Marriages, 1600 to the Present*, New York and Oxford, 1985, pp. 129–30.

10 British Library Collection 11602.gg.28.

11 British Library Collection 1876.e.3.

12 Old Bailey Sessions Papers 1771, p. 98; hereafter referred to as OBSP.

13 OBSP 1776–7, p. 387.

14 Dorothy George, *London Life in the Eighteenth Century*, Harmondsworth, Penguin, 1979 (1929), pp. 174, 207.

15 *The Autobiography of Francis Place*, ed. Mary Thrale, Cambridge University Press, 1972, pp. 71–3.

16 Gillis, *op. cit.*, pp. 101, 168.

17 Patrick Colquehoun, *A Treatise on the Police of the Metropolis* (London, 1797), p. 409.

18 Marybeth Hamilton, 'The Life of a Citizen in the Hands of a Woman: Sexual Assault in New York City, 1790–1820', Princeton University, 18 May 1984, unpublished paper, p. 23.

19 OBSP 1774, p. 396; see also OBSP 1773, p. 295.

20 Public Record Office, Chancery Lane, Assizes 45/30/2/122–3, 1 August 1772; hereafter referred to as PRO Assi. See also OBSP 1776 pp. 458–9.

21 Corporation of London Record Office, Mansion House Minute Books, 9 October 1790.

22 For the story of the squire and the milkmaid, versions include 'The Virtuous Milkmaid's Garland', British Library Collection L.R. 31.b.19; 'The Squire and the Milkmaid', Baring-Gould Collection, British Library; 'The Young Squire and Undaunted Mary', British Museum Collection 1875.d.5.

23 *The Genuine Trial of John Motherill . . . for a Rape on the Body of Miss Catherine Wade*, London, 1786, p. 3.

24 Paul-Gabriel Bouce, 'Some sexual beliefs and myths in 18th century Britain', in Paul-Gabriel Bouce (ed.), *Sexuality in 18th Century Britain*, Manchester University Press, 1982, p. 31.

25 OBSP 1781, p. 225.

26 OBSP 1771, p. 425.

27 PRO Assi.45/38/2/64–65 2 August 1794.

28 OBSP 1772–3, pp. 18–24, 42.

29 PRO Assi. 45/37/2/143, 20 April 1791.

30 OBSP 1781, p. 225.

31 OBSP 1796, p. 484ff.

32 OBSP 1777, p. 329.

33 PRO Assi. 45/35/3/27, 11 March 1786.

34 OBSP 1780, pp. 131–5.

35 OBSP 1784, p. 362.

36 OBSP October 1780, pp. 778ff.

37 OBSP 1780, pp. 778ff; OBSP 1771, p. 191; OBSP 1773, pp. 284–5; OBSP 1776, p. 297; and Corporation of London Record Office, Guildhall Justice Room Minute Book, 29

September 1780; Mansion House Minute Book, 28 May 1790.

38 Mansion House Minute Book, 28 May 1790; see also 27 July 1790.

39 PRO Ass. 45/30/2/150–151, 15 August 1772.

40 OBSP 1797, p. 250; see also OBSP 1796, p. 245, OBSP 1795, p. 59.

41 OBSP 1776–7, pp. 386–93; Guildhall Justice Room Minute Book, 28 August 1787; OBSP 1787, pp. 974ff, case of Wellen; OBSP 1787, pp. 954–9.

42 Homosexual prostitution did exist in eighteenth-century London but it was not as widespread as female prostitution, nor was it closely linked to economic distress. See Randolph Trumbach, 'London's Sodomites: Homosexual Behaviour and Western Culture in the 18th century', *Journal of Social History*, vol. 11, no. 1, Fall 1977, pp. 17–23. There were several prosecutions a year in the Middlesex Sessions Records for assault with intent to commit sodomy but it is difficult to discern if these were actual assaults or mutual acts interrupted by witnesses.

43 Manasseh Dawes, *An Essay on Crimes and Punishments* (London, 1782) pp. 85–90.

44 Joseph Gurney, *The Trial of John Motherill*, 2nd edn, London, 1786, p. 4.

45 Robert Bage, *Mount Henneth* (London, 1788), p. 187.

46 Peter Wagner, 'The pornographer in the courtroom: trial reports about cases of sexual crimes and delinquencies as a genre of 18th century erotica', in Paul-Gabriel Bouce (ed.), *Sexuality in 18th Century Britain*, Manchester University Press, 1982, p. 134.

47 See *The Trial of John Motherill the Brighton Tailor for a Rape in the Church Yard on the Body of Miss Catherine Wade*, London, 1806; John Motherill, *The Case of John Motherill, the Brighthelmstone Taylor who was tried at East Grinstead for a Rape . . . Written by Himself*, London, 1786.

48 For the term 'heroic rapist', see Brownmiller, chapter 9. *Fog's Weekly Journal*, quoted in Donna Lee Weber, 'Fair Game: Rape and Sexual Aggression in some early 18th century prose', University of Toronto Ph.D., 1980, p. 258. See also *Don Francisco's Descent to the Infernal Regions, an Interlude*, London, 1732; *Proceedings at the Sessions of the Peace . . . upon a Bill of Indictment found against Francis Charteris, Esq., for committing a Rape on the Body of Anne Bond, of which he was found guilty*; London, 1730, *Memories of the Life and Actions of Col. Ch—s, Rape-Master-General of Great Britain*, London, 1731; *The History of Col. Francis Ch–rtr–s . . .* 2nd edn, London, 1730.

49 *A Letter to Lord B—, with an Address to the Town*, London, 1768,

quoted in Weber, p. 256; see also *The Trial of Frederick Calvert, Lord Baltimore, for a Rape on the Body of Sarah Woodcock and of Elizabeth Griffinburg and Ann Harvey, otherwise Darby, as accessories*, London, 1768; *Observations on S. W———k's Own Evidence, Relative to the Pretended Rape*, London, 1768; *A Letter on the Behaviour of the Populace on a late occasion, in the procedure against a noble lord, from a Gentleman, to his countryman abroad*, London, 1768; [Rev. Bennet Allen], *Modern Chastity, or the Agreeable Rape*, London, 1768.

50 *A Curious Collection of Novels*, London, 1731, p. 40.

51 PRO Assi. 45/2/3/118–122, 4 August 1770.

52 OBSP 1780, pp. 131–5.

53 Motherill, p. 3.

54 *Rambler's Magazine*, January 1786, p. 6.

55 Samuel Richardson, *Clarissa*, London, 1759, vol. IV, pp. 494–5; *The Life and Death of John Carpenter [and others]*, London, 1805.

56 *Morning Herald*, 2 July 1803.

57 *Genuine Trial of John Motherill*, pp. 9–10.

58 *The Fond Mother's Garland*, London, 1770.

59 PRO Assi. 39/1/14, 23 July 1796.

60 PRO Assi. 45/43, 8 March 1807; see also PRO Assi. 45/34/2/3, 17 August 1781; PRO Assi. 45/38/1/93–98, 11 July 1793.

61 OBSP 1770, Williams and Taylor, 5 December.

62 Guildhall Justice Room Minute Books, 22 August 1787, and 24 February 1795, in City of London Corporation Record Office. There are many other cases in the minute books.

63 *Universal Register (The Times)* 22 April 1785.

64 PRO Assi. 45/39/1/69–71, 23 July 1796; PRO Assi. 45/36/2/92, 12 August 1789; PRO Assi. 45/36/2/140, March 1788; OBSP 1782, pp. 564–6.

65 OBSP 1772, pp. 214–15.

66 PRO Assi. 45/35/3/9, 11 March 1786.

67 Dawes, p. 91.

68 See also Carnemore case in Guildhall Justice Room Minute Books, 16 May 1794.

69 D. George, p. 250. For other cases of female apprentices being raped, Ruth K. McClure, in *Coram's Children: the London Foundling Hospital in the 18th Century*, New Haven and London, Yale University Press, 1981, p. 134, notes that in 1771 Sarah Drew, a foundling girl, reported that Job Wyatt, the woodscrew maker to whom she had been apprenticed, 'attempted to debauch her at 11 years of age and completed afterwards and continued the same ill-usage until Christmas last and beat her if she refused to submit to his will. That she was likewise informed her Master

had also debauched several other apprentices amongst whom were Mary Johnson, Mary Rise and Ann Beachamp who often talked of it to her.' The Governors of the Foundling Hospital ordered the girls discharged and bound to other masters. Another case of a master sexually abusing his female apprentices was reported in the *Universal Register* (which became *The Times*) 18 October 1785, involving a pinmaker.

70 OBSP 1772–3, p. 147.

71 OBSP 1786, pp. 1271–4.

72 J. Jean Hecht, *The Domestic Servant Class in 18th Century England*, London, Routledge & Kegan Paul, 1965, pp. 11, 87. Thanks to Margaret Hunt for illuminating this point.

73 OBSP 1770–2, p. 328; OBSP 1787 pp. 1168–9; see also OBSP 1774–5, p. 394.

74 *Universal Register (The Times)* 10 September 1789.

75 *Universal Register (The Times)* 24 October 1786; judge asks surgeon to refute this belief in OBSP 1796 pp. 304–7, OBSP 1796, pp. 787ff.

76 Weber, p. 259; Edward Bristow, *Vice and Vigilance: Purity Movements in Britain since 1700*, Totowa, NJ, Rowman & Littlefield, 1977, p. 60.

77 Middlesex Sessions Roll 3547, Indictment 29, 1792.

78 Greater London Record Office, London Consistory Court DL/C 179, Libel for divorce, 13 December 1781; for similar cases see also DL/C 290, Rea *v.* Rea, 1804; DL/C 281, Dickers *v.* Dickers, 1780; DL/C 282, Charlton *v.* Charlton, 1783.

79 DL/C 281, Emberson *v.* Emberson, 1780.

80 For women's fear of rape in fictional form, see Weber thesis: K. Ellis, 'Charlotte Smith's subversive gothic', *Feminist Studies* vol. 3, no. 3/4, Spring/Summer 1976, p. 55; Judith Lowder Newton, *Women, Power, and Subversion*, Athens, Georgia: University of Georgia Press, 1981; Terry Castle, 'Eros and Liberty at the English Masquerade, 1710–1790', *Eighteenth Century Studies*, vol. 17, no. 2, Winter 1983–4, p. 170.

81 *Midnight Rambler*, London, 1770, p. 95, and 'Advice to Constables, Watchmen, and Beadles', *Public Advertizer* 21 August 1790. Elizabeth Smith's father appeared in court when she was charged with picking up men (GJRMB, 4 July 1786); The Guildhall magistrate admonished Ann South at her mother's request because she 'led a bad life'. (GJRMB, 10 September 1794.) Mary Allen Collins was discharged to her mother who 'promised to keep her off the streets' and an alderman ordered her things to equip her for service, (GJRMB, 15 March 1796; see also 25 June 1786, 24 April 1794). The minute books are filled with cases of wifebeating.

82 Gurney, *Trial of John Motherill*, p. 4.
83 Jeffrey Weeks, *Sex, Politics, and Society: the Regulation of Sexuality since 1800*, London, Longmans, 1981, p. 84; thanks to Margaret Hunt for alerting me to the importance of these societies.
84 For radical views, see Marilyn Butler, *Jane Austen and the War of Ideas*, Oxford, Clarendon Press, 1975.

Chapter 3
A public shame: rape and eighteenth-century justice

1 Douglas Hay 'Property, Authority, and the Criminal Law', in D. Hay *et al.* (eds), *Albion's Fatal Tree*, London, Allen Lane, 1975; E.P. Thompson, *Whigs and Hunters: the Origins of the Black Acts*, London, Allen Lane, 1975, pp. 259–64.
2 Old Bailey Sessions Papers, 1777, pp. 321–32; OBSP 1778, pp. 75–81.
3 J.B. Post, 'Ravishment of Women and the Statutes of Westminster', in J.H. Baker (ed.), *Legal Records and the Historian*, Cambridge University Press, 1978; Nazife Bashar, 'Rape in England between 1550–1700' in London Feminist History Group (ed.), *The Sexual Dynamics of History: Men's Power, Women's Resistance*, London, Pluto Press, 1983, pp. 28–31.
4 Seven per cent from the Old Bailey Sessions, 1770–99; 13 per cent from North-east Assizes, 1770–1800; a quarter from Middlesex Sessions, 1770–5, 1780–5, 1790–5; 191 cases involved in the latter.
5 OBSP 1772–3, pp. 214–15.
6 OBSP 1775–6, pp. 411–12.
7 Susan Staves, 'British Seduced Maidens', *Eighteenth Century Studies*, vol. 14, no. 2, Winter 1980/1, pp. 109–34.
8 *Morning Herald*, 14 July 1803.
9 *Sun*, 14 April 1806, See also *The Times*, 16 August 1810, 21 July 1810.
10 John Fielding, *An Account of the Origin and Effects of the Police . . . to which is added a Plan for preserving those deserted Girls in this Town, who become Prostitutes from Necessity* (London, 1758), p. 45.
11 Nazife Bashar notes that rapes of children were also punished more severely and consistently in the seventeenth century (p. 38). Commenting on the punishment of rape in early Renaissance Venice, Guido Ruggiero writes that the fact that the

rape of female children (under the age of thirteen or fourteen) was punished much more severely than that of adult women refutes Phillipe Aries' thesis that in pre-modern times children were treated like miniature adults. Guido Ruggiero, *Violence in Early Renaissance Venice*, New Brunswick, N.J., Rutgers University Press, 1980, p. 165.

12 OBSP 1779, pp. 427–9. He was found not guilty.

13 *Folklore*, vol. 22, 1911, p. 237. Thanks to John Gillis for this reference.

14 Archives of the Count of Bedfordshire, QSR23, 1817, pp. 230–1, quoted in E.P. Thompson, 'Le Charivari anglais', *Annales E.S.C.*, 27, p. 305.

15 Martin Ingram, 'Ridings, Rough Music and the Reform of Popular Culture in Early Modern England', *Past and Present*, no. 105, November 1984, p. 91.

16 *Universal Register (The Times)*, 19 September 1788.

17 There are many examples of this in the magistrates minute books from 1770 to 1803 in the Corporation of London Record Office. See Guildhall Justice Room Minute Books 25 August 1794, 24 February 1795, 2 July 1792.

18 OBSP 1778, p. 78.

19 PRO Assi. 45/30/1/150–161. 1776.

20 PRO Assi. 45/38/2/85–87, 22 August 1794, PRO Assi. Minute Books 41/9.

21 OBSP 1776–7, p. 391. Found not guilty.

22 OBSP 1777, p. 288.

23 *Universal Register (The Times)*, 14 July 1786.

24 Middlesex Sessions Order Book, December 1777 (MJ/OC/10, pp. 166–89.

25 Henry Fielding, 'Rape upon Rape, or the Justice caught in his own trap', London, 1730, p. 10.

26 *Covent Garden Journal*, 2 May 1752.

27 *Morning Chronicle*, 30 August 1786.

28 Mansion House Minute Book, City of London Corporation Record Office, 22 January 1801.

29 In the Middlesex Sessions records, 15 per cent of attempted rape charges brought by adult women were dismissed by the magistrate and 18 per cent were dismissed by the Grand Jury, during the years 1770 to 75, 1780 to 85 and 1790 to 95. The figures for the North-east assizes were derived by tracing cases from the assizes minute books to the *Leeds Intelligencer*. For usual grand jury practice, see J.H. Baker, 'Criminal Courts and Procedure in the Common Law', in J.S. Cockburn, *Crime in England 1500–1800*, London, Methuen, 1977, p. 20.

30 Hay, *op cit.*
31 *Universal Register (The Times)*, 7 January 1788, also 7 November 1787. For cases where *The Times* dismisses the validity of rape cases, see 28 October 1790, 10 September 1789.
32 Bashar notes that the belief that a woman had to consent to sexual intercourse in order to conceive was a 'widely held legal dictum' in the seventeenth century. In the early nineteenth century, Samuel Farr continued to assert this notion, although he was the last to do so. See his *Elements of Medical Jurisprudence*, London, 1815, p. 45.
33 Edward Hyde East, *A Treatise on the Pleas of the Crown*, vol. I, London, 1803, pp. 437–40.
34 OBSP 1788, p. 699ff.
35 OBSP 1787 pp. 954–9.
36 OBSP, 1787, pp. 954–9.
37 OBSP, 1777, p. 328.
38 OBSP, 1778, p. 80.
39 OBSP, 1780, pp. 131–55.
40 OBSP, 1781, p. 226, OBSP, 1771, p. 231.
41 OBSP, 1780, pp. 181–5.
42 OBSP, 1773–5, pp. 222–5.
43 Nazife Bashar, *op. cit.*

Chapter 4
Silent suffering: law and medicine in the early nineteenth century

1 Nancy Cott, 'Passionlessness: An Interpretation of Victorian Sexual Ideology, 1790–1850', in N.F. Cott and E.H. Pleck (eds), *A Heritage of her Own: Toward a New Social History of American Women*, New York, Simon & Schuster, 1979, p. 167; also Catherine Hall, 'The Early Formation of Victorian Domestic Ideology' in Sandra Burman (ed.), *Fit Work for Women*, London, Croom Helm, 1979, p. 26.
2 Susan Edwards, *Female Sexuality and the Law*, Oxford, Martin Robertson, 1981.
3 Michel Foucault, *History of Sexuality*, vol. I, New York, Vintage Books, 1980. p. 10.
4 J. Chitty, *Practical Treatise in Medical Jurisprudence*, London, 1834, p. 379.
5 *Tables Showing the Number of Criminal Offenders in England and Wales* Parliamentary Papers 1841 (318) XVIII.255 and P.P. 1846 (701) XXXIV.1. For debates leading up to the removal of the death penalty for rape, see Hansard Parliamentary Debates, 3rd

series, vol. 58, Lords, 11 June 1841, Col. 1459, 14 June, Col. 1487.

6 The law which removed the requirement was 9 Geo. IV.c.31.s.16. For discussion of the change, see Chitty, p. 378.

7 Edwards, *op. cit.*, p. 120. For medical jurisprudence, see Robert Castel, 'The Doctors and Judges', in Michael Foucault (ed.), *I, Pierre Riviere* . . ., Harmondsworth, Penguin, 1975, p. 255.

8 Chitty p. 278.

9 Samuel Farr, *Elements of Medical Jurisprudence*, London, 1815, p. 45.

10 Farr, p. 45; T.R. Beck, *Elements of Medical Jurisprudence*, London, 1825, p. 57; A.S. Taylor, *A Manual of Medical Jurisprudence*, London, 1844, p. 579; Michael Ryan, *A Manual of Medical Jurisprudence*, London, 1831, p. 183.

11 Ryan, p. 181. See also Farr, p. 48.

12 *Morning Chronicle*, 29 July 1826.

13 *Morning Chronicle*, 3 August 1826.

14 *The Times*, 1 December 1836.

15 *The Times*, 20 December 1829.

16 PRO Assi. 45/55 Pt. 2, Spring 1822; see also Elliot case, PRO Assi. 45/56 Pt. 2, Summer Assizes, 1823 – Fentiman case.

17 PRO Assi. 45/43 5 August 1807.

18 *Weekly Dispatch*, 4 October 1834.

19 *The Times*, 5 September, 1840.

20 *Morning Chronicle*, 9 July 1834.

21 *Reynold's Newspaper*, 10 April 1853.

22 PRO Assi. 45/61 Pt. 2, 22 March 1828.

23 PRO Assi. 45/55 Pt. 2, 20 July 1822. See case of Irving, PRO Assi. 45/61, Pt., 3 March 1828, for a similar sentiment.

24 PRO Assi. 45/56, Yorkshire Summer Assi. 1823, PRO Assi. Minute Books 41/14, Guilty; see also the case of George Smith, whose victim threatened him unsuccessfully with the law. PRO Assi. 45/54, 4 August 1821. Case not prosecuted.

25 *The Times*, 13 October 1837.

26 *Weekly Dispatch*, 3 December 1843.

27 *Weekly Dispatch*, 17 May 1829.

28 *The Times*, 5 July 1844.

29 Michael Ignatieff, *A Just Measure of Pain: The Penitentiary in the Industrial Revolution*, New York: Columbia University Press, 1980, p. 133.

30 *The Times*, 2 April 1829. See also *Leeds Intelligencer*, 23 July 1819, which reports that Elizabeth Senthouse was imprisoned in lieu of sureties to appear to prosecute her master's son for rape. There were also cases in which male prosecutors were

imprisoned. For instance, a foreigner who accused a prostitute of robbing him in a brothel was imprisoned in lieu of sureties in 1831. *Morning Chronicle*, 15 July 1831.

31 *Leeds Intelligencer*, 2 August 1819, also PRO Assi. 45/52 Pt. 1, 24 Jly 1819, PRO Minute Books 41/12, Not guilty.

32 *The Times*, 27 August 1821.

33 *The Times*, 9 August 1824. PRO Assi. 45/57, PRO minute books 41/4.

34 *Morning Chronicle*, 29 December 1829, 9 January 1829, 7 December 1829, 31 July 1829.

35 Charles Hindley, *Curiosities of Street Literature*, Vol. II, Leslie Shepard (ed.), London, the Broadsheet King, 1956.

36 Sabine Baring-Gould Collection of Ballads, British Library.

37 *Weekly Dispatch*, 12 October 1834.

38 *Weekly Dispatch*, 25 September 1825; see also *Weekly Dispatch*, 5 January 1833; *The Times*, 9 October 1817; *The Times*, 21 July 1834, *Weekly Dispatch*, 11 April 1821, for similar reports which blame the victim.

39 In her article 'The "Maiden Tribute of Modern Babylon" re-examined: child prostitution and the idea of childhood in late-Victorian England', *Victorian Studies* vol. 21, no. 3, Spring 1978, p. 370, Deborah Gorham discusses the 'two powerful but opposed images of . . . the child as redeemer and the child as evil incarnate', the former stemming from Evangelical imagery and the latter from Calvinist theology.

40 Ryan, pp. 183, 191, 1832. In 1828 attempted rape of children was made a capital felony. This was known as the Law of Lord Landsdowne. For further discussion of later developments in medical jurisprudence about child rape, see the discussions of French medical jurisprudence in Chapter Two of Jeffrey Moussaieff Masson's *Assault on Truth: Freud's Suppression of the Seduction Theory*, Harmondsworth, Penguin, 1985. Masson notes that two opposing traditions developed in this field: one, represented by Ambrose Tardieu and Paul Bernard, presented medical evidence about the widespread, and very violent, sexual assault of children, while Paul Brouardel tried to assert (in the face of such medical evidence) that such children were lying.

41 *The Times*, 7 January 1830.

42 *Weekly Dispatch*, 31 May 1835; *Weekly Dispatch*, 26 March 1837; *Weekly Dispatch*, 22 March 1835.

43 A.S. Taylor, p. 575.

44 *The Times*, 12 December 1843.

45 *The Times*, 20 December 1819.

46 *Weekly Dispatch*, 1 March 1829.

47 Edward Hyde East, *A Treatise on the Pleas of the Crown*, Vol. I, London, 1803, p. 44.

48 Jean L'Esperance, 'Doctors and Women in 19th Century Society: Sexuality and Role' in J. Woodward and D. Richards (eds), *Health Care and Popular Medicine in 19th Century England*, London, Croom Helm, 1977, p. 114. See also Eric Trudgill, *Madonnas and Magdalens: The Origins and Development of Victorian Sexual Attitudes*, London, Heinemann, 1976, pp. 55–6; and F. Barry Smith, 'Sexuality in Britain, 1800–1900: Some Suggested Revisions,' in Martha Vicinus (ed.), *A Widening Sphere*, London and Bloomington, Ind., Indiana University Press, 1977.

49 *The Times*, 29 October 1829.

50 *The Times*, 2 March 1838.

51 *The Times*, 1 August 1836.

52 *Weekly Dispatch*, 29 October 1843.

53 *The Times*, 21 March 1838.

54 Farr, p. 45; T.R. Beck, *Elements of Medical Jurisprudence*, London, 1825, p. 57; A.S. Taylor, *A Manual of Medical Jurisprudence*, London, 1844, p. 579; Michael Ryan, *A Manual of Medical Jurisprudence*, London, 1831, p. 183.

55 Ryan, p. 182.

56 John Hall (ed.), *The Trial of Abraham Thornton*, Notable British Trial Series, London and Edinburgh, William Hodge and Co., 1926, p. 98.

57 *Ibid.*, pp. 78–9.

58 Lorenne Clark and Debra J. Lewis, *Rape: the Price of Coercive Sexuality*, Toronto, the Women's Press, 1977, pp. 120–1.

59 East, *op. cit.*, p. 444.

60 Quoted in Edwards, *op. cit.*, p. 63.

61 Quoted in H.A. Snelling, 'What is Rape' in L. Schultz (ed.), *Rape Victimology*, Springfield IL, Charles C. Thomas, 1975, p. 153.

62 Delia Dumaresq, 'Rape – Sexuality in the Law', *m/f* Nos. 5 and 6, 1981, p. 44.

63 *The Times*, 3 August 1844.

64 *The Times*, 10 April 1837.

65 *The Times*, 8 April 1841.

66 *The Times*, 20 August 1824.

67 Edwards, *op. cit.*, pp. 136–7.

Chapter 5
Middle-class myths, working-class realities

1 J. Brownlow, *Memoranda, or Chronicles of the Foundling Hospital* (London, 1847), p. 194.
2 *Ibid.*, p. 192.
3 John Gillis, 'Servants, Sexual Relations, and the Risk of Illegitimacy in London, 1801–1900', *Feminist Studies*, vol. 5, no. 1, Spring 1979, p. 146.

   The petitions studied in this chapter are from 1815 to 1845. I sampled one in three of both accepted and rejected petitions, for a total of 1,040 petitions. Due to archival regulations, the name of the Foundling Hospital has not been mentioned in the text, and the names of all petitioners have been changed.
4 Foundling Hospital petitions 1844 – accepted – 107; FH 1839 – accepted – unnumbered.; FH 1844 – rejected – 195; 1844 – accepted – 182; 1816 – accepted – unnumbered.
5 J. Brownlow, 'An Appeal to the Benevolent' (London, n.d.).
6 Jean L'Esperance, 'Doctors and Women in 19th Century Society: Sexuality and Role' in J. Woodward and D. Richards (eds), *Health Care and Popular Medicine in 19th Century England*, London, Croom Helm, 1977, p. 114.
7 FH 1833 – accepted – unnumbered.
8 FH 1844 – rejected – 184.
9 FH 1838 – rejected – 120; 1842 – accepted – 146; 1841 – accepted – unnumbered.
10 Gillis, *op. cit.*, p. 146.
11 Gillis discusses these issues in depth. For prebridal pregnancy, P.E. Hair cites a figure of forty-nine pregnant brides out of every hundred women married in Medmenham, Bucks., between 1750 and 1836 ('Bridal Pregnancy', *Population Studies* 24 (1970), p. 62). Carol Pearce gives a 38.2 per cent figure for Ashford, Kent, during the mid-nineteenth century ('Some Aspects of Fertility in a Mid-Victorian Community', *Local Population Studies* 10, Spring 1973, p. 25.
12 Barbara Taylor, *Eve and the New Jerusalem: Socialism and Feminism in the 19th Century*, New York, Pantheon, 1983, p. 194.
13 Gillis, *op. cit.*, p. 155.
14 Madden Collection of Ballads, Cambridge University Library.
15 *Aristotle's Masterpiece* (London, 1771), p. 38. See also 1749 edn.
16 *Aristotle's Masterpiece* (London, 1812), p. 32.
17 Gillis, *op. cit.*, p. 157.
18 *Poor Man's Guardian* 24 May 1834.

19 Taylor, *op. cit.*, pp. 195–205.
20 *London City Mission Magazine* vol. 5, no. 110, July 1840, p. 106.
21 Janet Blackman, 'Popular Theories of Generation: the Evolution of *Aristotle's Works*' in J. Woodward and D. Richards (eds), *Health Care and Popular Medicine in 19th Century England*, London, Croom Helm, 1977, p. 69.
22 Taylor, *op. cit.*, pp. 207–13.
23 Gillis, *op. cit.*, p. 158.
24 Susan Staves, 'British Seduced Maidens', *Eighteenth Century Studies* vol. 14, no. 2, Winter 1980/1, p. 108; William Cobbett, *Advice to Young Men (and Incidentally to Young Women in the Middle and Higher Ranks of Life* (London, 1829) III, no. 90.
25 FH 1843 – rejected – 83.
26 Gillis, *op. cit.*, p. 156; FH 1823 – accepted – unnumbered.
27 FH 1844 – accepted – 12.
28 FH 1825 – accepted – 8.

Chapter 6
The daughters of poor men: radical rhetoric, women's experience

1 For a further discussion of this theme, see my article, 'The Politics of Seduction' in *The Progress of Romance*, edited by Jean Radford, History Workshop Series, London, Routledge & Kegan Paul, 1986.
2 From an unlabelled newspaper clipping in the Francis Place Collection, vol. 56, British Library, London. Anti-Poor Law meeting at Bradford, *c.* 1834–44.
3 Allen Davenport, *Life of Thomas Spence*, 1839, p. 22, quoted in Judith R. Walkowitz, *Prostitution and Victorian Society*, Cambridge, Cambridge University Press, 1980, p. 35.
4 For incidents of sexual coercion in workhouses, see the following: Sheffield workhouse, in Samuel Roberts, *Truth, or the Fall of Babylon the Great, being an address . . . on the Poor Law Amendment Act*, Sheffield, 1845, pp. 25–9; Southwell, Notts., London, Public Record Office, Poor Law correspondence, MH 12 9525, 16 July 1838; Hoo Union, *The Times*, 25 March 1835; Andover Workhouse, Ian Anstruther, *The Scandal of the Andover Workhouse: A Documentary Study of Events 1834–1847*, London, Geoffrey Bles, 1973, p. 131; Bath Union, *The Times*, 25 November 1840; South Moulton workhouse, *Weekly Dispatch*, 28 February 1841. Children and young women were also vulnerable to sexual assault by gang masters in the gang system of agricultural labour. See Ivy Pinchbeck and Margaret Hewitt,

Children in English Society, vol. II, London, Routledge & Kegan Paul, 1973, p. 393. There were many instances of rape in lunatic asylums. See Elaine Showalter, 'Victorian Women and Insanity', *Victorian Studies* (1980) p. 320.

5 For sexual coercion in needlework establishments, in one incident a foreman assaulted a waistcoat-maker when she brought work to be checked (*Weekly Dispatch*, 1 August 1841) and a slopseller and tailor assaulted a young women who worked for him (*Weekly Dispatch*, 10 May 1835).

6 Barbara Taylor, *Eve and the New Jerusalem: Socialism and Feminism in the Nineteenth Century*, New York, Pantheon, 1983, p. 274.

7 Noted in Louis James, *Print and the People, 1819–1851*, Harmondsworth, Penguin, 1978, pp. 116–17.

8 *Report on the bill to regulate the Labour of Children in Factories and Mills*, Parliamentary Papers 1831–2, XV, p. 454. Hereafter cited as 1831–2 Report.

9 *The Times*, 10, 11 September 1824.

10 1833 Report, p. 339.

11 Ivy Pinchbeck, *Women Workers in the Industrial Revolution, 1750–1850*, London, Virago, 1981 (1930), p. 146.

12 PRO Assizes 45/55 Pt. 1, 29 December 1821. He was found not guilty but prosecuted for a misdemeanour, PRO Assize Minute Books, 41/12.

13 PRO Assizes 45/55 Pt. 1, 30 January 1822; found not guilty, PRO Assizes Minute Books 41/12; PRO Assizes 45/54, 10 March 1821; found guilty of assault, committed to five years in gaol. PRO Assizes Minute Books 41/12. There were no cases of boys sexually assaulted in mills found in the assize records.

14 *Leeds Intelligencer*, 12 October 1839.

15 *Leeds Intelligencer*, 21 October 1843, 6 January 1844.

16 *Leeds Intelligencer*, 18 January 1834.

17 Factory Inquiry Committee, *Report of the Commissioners*, Parliamentary Papers 1833 XX p. 417. Hereafter cited as 1833 Report.

18 1831–2 Report, pp. 417, 131.

19 *Northern Star*, 3 March 1838; see also *Leeds Intelligencer*, 27 February 1841.

20 *Leeds Intelligencer*, 15 June 1833.

21 1831–2 Report, p. 89.

22 *Ibid.*, p. 47.

23 1833 Report, pp. 421, 426.

24 Francis Place, letter to Harriet Martineau, 8 September 1832, in Francis Place, *Illustrations and Proofs of the Principle of*

Population, edited by N.E. Himes, London, George Allen & Unwin, 1930, p. 326.

25 Dorothy Thompson, 'Women and 19th century radical politics: the lost dimension', in J. Mitchell and A. Oakley (eds), *The Rights and Wrongs of Women*, Harmondsworth, Penguin, 1976, p. 130; Pinchbeck, pp. 199–200.

26 David Phillips, *Crime and Authority in Victorian England: The Black Country, 1835–1860*, London, Croom Helm, 1977, p. 152.

27 *Northern Star*, 3 March 1838.

28 *Leeds Intelligencer*, 15 June 1833.

29 Joseph Lawson, *Progress in Pudsey*, Stanningley, 1887, p. 58. Thanks to Sian Moore for this reference.

30 *Leeds Intelligencer*, 12 March 1836.

31 PRO Assizes 45/62 Pt. 2, Westmoreland, Lent Assizes 1829; PRO Assi. 45/62 Pt. 1, 21 March 1829. For a similar case of workers raping a co-worker's wife, in this case stuffpressers, see PRO Assi. 45/39/3/75, 21 July 1798, case of T. Hill, J. Holmesby, and J. Birch.

32 David Finkelhor, *Sexually Victimized Children*, New York, Free Press/Macmillan, 1979, pp. 4, 62.

33 Anthony Wohl, 'Sex in the Single Room: Incest among the Victorian Working Class', in A. Wohl (ed.), *The Victorian Family*, London, Croom Helm, 1978, p. 203. Wohl however dismisses most concern over incest as middle-class anxiety.

34 PRO Assizes 45/62 Pt. 1, Lent Assizes 1829; found guilty, fourteen months hard labour, PRO Assizes Minute Books 41/14.

35 PRO Assizes 45/49, 9 March 1815.

36 *Northern Star*, 2 May 1840.

37 *New Rambler's Magazine*, n.d., vol. II, pp. 193–4. Child prostitution, while not as widespread as reformers alleged, did exist. See Hilary Evans, *Harlots, Whores, and Hookers: A History of Prostitution*, New York, Taplinger Publications, 1979, p. 127.

38 *Weekly Dispatch*, 29 January 1843.

39 *Weekly Dispatch*, 22 November 1840; for another similar incident, see *Cosmopolite*, 24 November 1832.

40 *Weekly Dispatch*, 19 April 1835.

41 Finkelhor, p. 5. Incest was an underground theme in eighteen-century and early nineteenth-century popular literature. Some radicals used it to critique old institutions as outmoded and exploitative: see Peter Thorsler, 'Incest as a Romantic Symbol', *Comparative Literature Studies*, vol. 2, 1965, pp. 42–7. But predatory, incestuous father figures in literature may have also drawn upon women's personal fears. For an example of an aged aristocratic rogue pursuing the heroine and being unmasked as

her father, see the anonymous popular novel, *Seduction*, London, 1848. For an example of an incestuous uncle, see M.G. Lewis, *The Castle Spectre*, Lacy's Acting Edition, Vol. XV; for a novel concerning pursuit by a father figure, the father of the heroine's lover, see Anonymous, *The Adventures of Sylvia Hughes*, New York, Garland, 1975 (1761). In T.P. Prest's *Emily Fitzormond*, London, 1842, the orphan heroine fears that her mysterious, aged and lascivious guardian is her father: '. . . perhaps that wretch, that miscreant, was her father? . . . Was it possible that the hoary-headed man, who affected so much kindness and benevolence, should contemplate the violation of a poor, deserted, friendless, girl, to whom he was old enough to be a grandfather?' (pp. 140–1). Mary Shelley deliberately used the theme of incest in her unpublished novel *Mathilda*, drawing upon literary precedents. See Elizabeth Nitchie, introduction to *Mathilda*, in *Studies in Philology*, extra series, October 1959, vol. 3.

42 Linda Gordon and Paul O'Keefe, 'Incest as a form of family violence: evidence from historical case records', *Journal of Marriage and the Family*, February 1984, p. 31.

43 Robert Roberts, *The Classic Slum: Salford Life in the First Quarter of the 20th Century*, Harmondsworth, Penguin, 1973, p. 44 (quoted in John Gillis, *For Better, for Worse: British Marriages 1600 to the Present*, New York and Oxford, Oxford University Press, 1985, p. 265) notes that the matriarchs of his Salford neighbourhood punished incest themselves.

44 *Weekly Dispatch*, 24 August 1845.

45 PRO Assizes 45/44, 30 July 1808; found not guilty, PRO Assizes Minute Books 41/11.

46 Judith Herman with Lisa Hirschman, *Father-Daughter Incest*, Cambridge, Mass., Harvard University Press, 1981, pp. 48, 62; Finkelhor, *op. cit.*, p. 207.

47 Ivy Pinchbeck and Margaret Hewitt, *Children in English Society*, Vol II, London, Routledge & Kegan Paul, 1973, pp. 368–9.

48 PRO Assize 45/46 Pt. 2; 25 August 1813; found not guilty, PRO Assize Minute Books 41/11.

49 Herman, *op. cit.*, p. 48; Gordon and O'Keefe, *op. cit.*, p. 30.

50 *Weekly Dispatch*, 17 January 1836. See also an incident in which James Sullivan, a labourer separated from his wife, raped his fourteen-year-old illegitimate daughter. He was convicted to two years hard labour. *Weekly Dispatch*, 5 March 1843; Joseph Wilson's wife had died before he assaulted his daughter. *Weekly Dispatch*, 21 September 1821. A man named Leverett assaulted his daughter when his wife was absent. *The Times*, 7 December

1823; another widower, a soldier, accused of assaulting his daughter, *Weekly Dispatch*, 28 June 1835; James Macdonald separated from his wife, *The Times*, 2 November 1827; see also *The Times*, 6 December 1827, *The Times*, 2 November 1827.

51 *Northern Star*, 6 August 1842.

52 *Weekly Dispatch*, 27 May 1838.

53 *Weekly Dispatch*, 21 September 1823.

54 *Weekly Dispatch*, 11 October 1831.

55 Incest did not become illegal in England until 1908. Jeffrey Weeks, *Sex, Politics and Society: The Regulation of Sexuality since 1800*, London, Longman, 1981, p. 31.

56 *Weekly Dispatch*, 21 April 1839; *Weekly Dispatch*, 24 November 1832.

57 Gordon and O'Keefe, *op. cit.*, p. 30.

58 *Weekly Dispatch*, 22 April 1827.

59 *Leeds Intelligencer*, 31 March 1817. Other material on this case found in PRO Assize 45/50 Pt. 1, Hull, 8 March 1817, found not guilty in PRO Assize Minute Books 41/11.

60 *The Diaries of Hannah Cullwick: Victorian Maidservant*, edited and introduced by Liz Stanley, London, Virago, 1984, pp. 31–2.

61 P.W. Razzell and R.W. Wainwright, *The Victorian Working Class: Selections from Letters to the Victorian Chronicle*, London, Cassells, 1973, pp. 296–7.

62 Pinchbeck, *Women Workers*, pp. 37–40.

63 PRO Assizes 45/55 Pt. 2; 20 July 1822.

64 PRO Assizes 45/52 Pt. 1, 24 July 1819; found guilty, PRO Assizes minute books 41/12.

65 *The Times*, 21 February 1835.

66 *Weekly Dispatch*, 11 May 1845.

67 *The Times*, 7 November 1827.

68 *The Times*, 12 October 1827.

69 *The Diaries of Hannah Cullwick*, p. 43.

70 Leonore Davidoff, 'Class and Gender in Victorian England: the Diaries of Arthur J. Munby and Hannah Cullwick', *Feminist Studies* vol. V, 1979, p. 105.

71 John Gillis, 'Servants, Sexual Relations, and the Risk of Illegitimacy in London, 1801–1900', *Feminist Studies* vol. V, 1979, p. 156.

72 Foundling Hospital Petition 1835 – accepted – 90.

73 Foundling Hospital Petition 1829 – accepted – 46.

74 See Leonore Davidoff, 'Mastered for Life: Servant and Wife in Victorian England', *Journal of Social History*, vol. 7, 1974, pp. 406–28.

Chapter 7
Rape as warning: the genesis of a middle-class myth

1 Broadsheet, 'Confession, though not the Dying Speech of Abraham Thornton, ca. 1817', from Nottingham City Library Broadsheet Collection.
2 Leonore Davidoff and Catherine Hall, 'The Separation of Spheres, 1780–1850: Birmingham and East Anglia, Two Case Studies.' Interim report, University of Essex, 1980, unpublished.
3 Derek Hudson, *Munby: Man of Two Worlds*, London, Sphere, 1974, p. 99. Although this quote is from the 1860s, similar scenes could be seen in London in the early part of the century.
4 *The Times*, 16 September 1824.
5 For melodramas, see S.N.E., 'The Murdered Maid', Warwick, 1818, and [G. Ludlam], 'The Mysterious Murder, or What's the Clock', 2nd edn, Birmingham, *c.* 1818. *Trial by Battle, or Heaven Defend the Right* was performed at the Cobourg Theatre (later the Victoria) in May 1818; a performance of this play also closed the theatre on 9 September 1871; see H. Barton Baker, *The London Stage*, London, 1889. Thanks to Raphael Samuel for this reference. For pamphlets on London streets, see *Horrible Rape and Murder! The Affecting Case of Mary Ashford . . .* , London, 1817. Charles Hindley, in *The Life and Times of James Catnach*, Welywyn Garden City, Herts, Seven Dials Press, 1970 (1878) p. 358, notes that hawkers used lurid posters to sell pamphlets about Mary Ashford in the mid-nineteenth century. For ballads, 'Mary Ashford's Tragedy', 'The Sorrowful Lamentation of Mary Ashford's True Lover', 'A new song on the ghost of Mary Ashfield appearing to Abraham Thorntree', and 'Mary Ashford', all printed in Birmingham, in the Madden Collection, Cambridge University Library, and also 'Elegy, written on the Murder of Mary Ashford' in the John Johnson Collection, Crime Section, box 12, Bodleian Library, Oxford University. The case of Abraham Thornton excited attention not only for its sexual aspects but because Mary Ashford's young brother invoked an obscure legal precedent to appeal the acquittal, and Thornton responded by asking to prove his innocence through a 'Wager of Battle', i.e. challenging the brother to a fight.
6 Testimony of John Hompidge, in John Hall (ed.), *The Trial of Abraham Thornton*, London and Edinburgh, William Hodge and Col, 1926, p. 72.
7 *The Times*, 19 August 1824.
8 'The Murdered Maid', pp. 12–13.

9 The Rev. Luke Booker, *A Moral Review of the Conduct and Case of Mary Ashford* . . . , Dudley, 1818, p. 26.

10 Edward Holroyd, *Observations on the Case of Abraham Thornton*, London, 1819, pp. 24, 87.

11 'The Murdered Maid', p. 43.

12 'Attorney at Law', *An Investigation into the Case of Mary Ashford*, London, 1818, pp. 16–18.

13 *Ladies Monthly Museum*, March 1818, pp. 121–6.

14 'The Murdered Maid', p. 22.

15 Booker, p. 10. The *Gentlemen's Magazine* assented to Booker's warnings to young women to stay and home and preserve their modesty. June 1818, p. 535.

16 'Friend to Justice', *Reply to the Remarks of the Rev. Luke Booker*, Birmingham, 1818, p. 34.

17 'Mary Ashford's Tragedy', printed in Birmingham, in Madden Collection, Cambridge University Library; see also a similar warning ballad, 'Elegy, written on the Murder of Mary Ashford' in the John Johnson Collection, Crime Section, box 12, Bodleian Library, Oxford University.

18 *The Times*, 1 October 1823.

19 *Diary*, 31 May 1791, in Miss S. Bank's Collection of Cuttings, British Library, which contains copious clippings and pamphlets on 'The Monster'; see also an account of similar attacks in *The True Briton*, 25 February 1797.

20 *The Times*, 9 December 1839; see also a case in which a Mr Kelly, an auctioneer at West Smithfield, tried to decide whether to press charges against a confectioner who had assaulted his nineteen-year-old daughter. She had been going about her father's business, accompanied by a servant. He said 'he was desirous of sparing the feelings of his daughter, which would be much agonized in describing in a court of a justice the indecent particulars of the assault committed on her.' (*The Times*, 1 October 1823). When a Mrs Inman charged George Dent, 'a respectable-looking young man . . . with taking liberties with her and assaulting her on Waterloo Road', she had to explain to the magistrate that 'she was a married woman, but that her husband was prevented from attending in consequence of illness.' (*The Times*, 16 July 1838). At that time Waterloo Road had many brothels.

21 *The Times*, 11 March 1826.

22 *Weekly Dispatch*, 20 September 1840; *The Times*, 13 July 1824; *The Times*, 14 September 1844; *Weekly Dispatch*, 17 December 1843.

23 *Weekly Dispatch*, 2, 9, 16 August 1840. Christine Stansell has

described a similar phenomenon in early nineteenth-century New York City: young working-class men imitated the disorderly behaviour of Regency dandies or bloods. See the introduction to her book, *Women of the Poor in Federalist and Early National New York*, forthcoming.

24 'Walter', *My Secret Life*, New York, Grove, 1966, abridged edition; throughout the entire book he accosts working-class women for sexual services. Testimony of unmarried mothers to the London Foundling Hospital also indicates that their seducers often accosted them on the streets and followed them home.

25 *The Times*, 30 March 1830.

26 *The Times*, 15 June 1827.

27 *Universal Register (The Times)*, 22 April 1785.

28 Francis Shepherd, *London 1808–1870: The Infernal Wen*, Berkeley, University of California, 1971, p. 84.

29 Eric Trudgill, 'Prostitution and Paterfamilias', in H.J. Dyos and M. Wolff (eds), *The Victorian City*, Vol. II, London, Routledge & Kegan Paul, 1973.

30 Patrick Colquhoun, *A Treatise on the Police of the Metropolis*, London, 1797, pp. vii–xi, 409, 414, 438. For works on the introduction of the New Police, see T.A. Critchley, *The History of the Police in England and Wales 900–1960*, London, Constable, 1967, revised 1978; Tony Bunyan, *The History and Practice of the Political Police and Britain*, London, Julian Friedman, 1976; for resistance to the police see Robert Storch, 'A Plague of Blue Locusts': Police Reform and Popular Resistance in Northern England 1840–1857', *International Review of Social History*, vol. 20, 1975, 79–89.

31 *The Times*, 10 October 1836.

32 Colquhoun, p. 342.

33 When Mrs Elizabeth Luckie, the 'wife of a respectable carpenter', appealed to a constable for help in chasing her 'unmanly assailant', he laid hold of her arm, and 'pinching it with great violence, exclaimed, I tell you what marm, if you are not quiet, I shall pretty soon lock you up; we're not going to have any of your rows here.' *The Times*, 27 July 1824. In 1829 *The Times* cited the case of a woman who was molested in a watchhouse after she sought shelter there to criticize the 'substitute constables' who preceded the professional police force. *The Times*, 2 May 1829.

34 *Weekly Dispatch*, 20 August 1840.

35 *The Times*, 27 October 1836; see also *The Times*, 16 July 1828.

36 *Weekly Dispatch*, 11 June 1837.

37 *Weekly Dispatch*, 30 April 1837.

38 *Weekly Dispatch*, 10 November 1844; see also *Weekly Dispatch*, 18 July 1841, when Dennis Power, police serjeant was fined three pounds for 'a brutal assault on an unfortunate woman, against whom he attempted to trump up an unfounded charge'; and *Lloyd's Weekly Newspaper*, 4 August 1844, which reports that P.C. Michael Maguier was charged with entering the house of eighteen-year-old Emma Moody, and molesting her in her bed.
39 *Weekly Dispatch*, 5 November 1843.
40 *Weekly Dispatch*, 26 July 1840; *The Times*, 18 December 1829.
41 *The Times*, 8 August 1834.
42 *The Times*, 1 December 1836.
43 Broadsheet entitled 'The Extraordinary Life and Death of Mary Anne Pierce' in John Johnson Collection, Murders and Executions, Vol. 3, Bodleian Library, Oxford University.
44 *Weekly Dispatch*, 4 October 1840, 11 October 1840; Judith Walkowitz notes the use by prostitutes of rough music to resist police in her *Prostitution and Victorian Society: Women, Class, and the State*, Cambridge University Press, 1981, p. 27.
45 *The Times* and *Sun*, 13 December 1827.
46 *The Times* and *Sun*, 17 December 1827.
47 *Jackson's Oxford Journal*, 22 December 1827.
48 *The Times*, 24 December 1827.
49 *The Times*, 26 December 1827.
50 *The Times*, 31 December 1827.

Chapter 8
Conclusion

1 T.P. Prest, *Emily Fitzormond*, London, 1842, pp. 140–1.
2 Sally Mitchell, 'The Forgotten Female of the Period: Penny Weekly Family Magazines of the 1830s and 1840s' in Martha Vicinus (ed.), *A Widening Sphere*, Bloomington, Ind., Indiana University Press, 1978, p. 43.
3 Associate Institution for Improving and Enforcing the Laws for Protection of Women, *Remedies for the Wrongs of Women*, London, 1844, p. 33.
4 Committee of the London Female Penitentiary, *Report*, London, 1836, pp. 15–16.
5 London Rape Crisis Centre, *Sexual Violence: the Reality for Women*, London, The Women's Press, 1984, p. 2.
6 Polly Pattullo, *Judging Women*, London, National Council for Civil Liberties, 1983, p. 21.
7 Wendy Holloway, 'I just wanted to kill a woman. Why? The

ripper and male sexuality', *Feminist Review*, no. 9, Autumn 1981, p. 35.

8 London Rape Crisis Centre, p. 40.

9 National Council for Civil Liberties, p. 21.

10 Susan Edwards, *Female Sexuality and the Law*, Oxford, Martin Robinson, 1981, p. 126.

11 *Outwrite*, Issue 25, May 1984, p. 4.

12 Edwards, *op. cit.*, pp. 101–11.

13 Judith Herman, *Father-Daughter Incest*, Cambridge, Mass., Harvard University Press, 1981, p. 11. See also Jeffrey Moussaieff Masson, *The Assault on Truth: Freud's Suppression of the Seduction Theory*, Harmondsworth, Penguin, 1985.

14 London Rape Crisis Centre, p. 31.

15 Judith Walkowitz, *Prostitution and Victorian Society: Women, Class and State*, Cambridge, Cambridge University Press, 1980.

16 Judith Walkowitz, 'Jack the Ripper and the Myth of Male Violence', *Feminist Studies*, vol. 8, no. 3 (Fall, 1982) 543–74.

17 Sheila Jeffreys, 'Free from all uninvited touch of man: women's campaigns around sexuality, 1880–1914', *Women's Studies International Forum*, 5 June 1982. Elizabeth Pleck also cites the Chicago Protective Agency for Women and Children, founded in 1885 by women's organizations, which aided women and children who had been victimized by sexual assault and served as their advocates in court. After eleven years, it merged with a male bureau and lost its feminist impact. 'Feminist response to crimes against women, 1868–1896', *Signs*, vol. 8, no. 3, Spring 1983, p. 466.

18 Jan Lambertz, 'Sexual Harassment in the 19th-century English Cotton Industry', *History Workshop Journal*, 19, Spring 1985, pp. 29–61.

19 Linda Gordon and Ellen Dubois, 'Seeking Ecstasy on the Battlefield: Danger and Pleasure in 19th century feminist thought', in Carole Vance (ed.), *Pleasure and Danger: Exploring Female Sexuality*, Boston, Routledge & Kegan Paul, 1984, p. 33.

Select bibliography

Major primary sources

Manuscript sources:
London, Greater London Council Record Office
　Foundling Hospital Collection:
　Petitions 1815–1845, accepted and rejected.
　Middlesex Sessions Papers, 1770–1775, 1780–1785, 1790–1795.
London, Public Record Office, Chancery Lane
　Assizes Depositions and Minute Books
　North-East Circuit, 1770–1829.
London, Corporation of the City of London Record Office
　Magistrates' Minute Books, 1780–1804.

Collections:
London, British Library
　Collection of Ballads by Sabine-Baring Gould.
　Compton Collection of Ballads.
　Miss S. Banks' Collection of Cuttings.
　Francis Place Collection of Cuttings.
　Francis Place Additional Manuscripts.
　Miscellaneous Collections Call Numbers 1875.d.5; 1881.d.8; N.
　　Tab. 2021/28; L.R. 271.a.2; L.R. 31.b.19; 11643.bbb.43.1–6;
　　C.116.i.1; 1876.c.3; 1875.d.13; Cup.407.mm.29.
Cambridge, University Library
　Madden Collection of Ballads.
Oxford, Bodleian Library
　John Johnson Collection.
Nottingham, Local History Library
　Collection of Ballads.
London, St Bride's Library of Printing
　Collection of Song Sheets and Catchpennies.

Parliamentary Papers:
'Report from the Select Committee on the Police of the Metropolis.'
   PP 1828 (533) VI.1.
'Report on the Bill to Regulate the Labour of Children in Factories
   and Mills.' PP 1831–2, XV.
'Report of Commissioners, Factory Inquiry Committee.' PP 1833
   XX.
'Report of the State of Children in Manufacture.' PP 1816.III.

Old Bailey Sessions Papers. Printed transcripts, 1770–1800.

Periodicals:
Bell's Life of London
Cleave's Police Gazette
Cosmopolite
Covent Garden Journal
Gentleman's Magazine
Hetherington's Twopenny Dispatch
Independent Whig
Jackson's Oxford Journal
Ladies Monthly Museum
The Leeds Intelligencer
The Leeds Mercury
*Lloyd's Companion to the Penny Sunday Times and People's Police
   Gazette*
Lloyd's Weekly London Newspaper
London Chronicle
Morning Herald
Morning Chronicle
The Northern Star
Observer
Public Advertizer
Reynold's News
Sun
The Times
True Briton
Weekly Dispatch

Selected secondary sources

This list is intended to aid those who wish to do further reading in
this field.

Alexander, Sally, 'Women's Work in 19th Century London' in

J. Mitchell and A. Oakley (eds), *The Rights and Wrongs of Women*, Harmondsworth, Penguin, 1976.

Barnett, H.C. 'Political Economy of Rape and Prostitution', *Review of Radical Political Economy*, vol. 8, no. 1, 1976, 39–66.

Bashar, Nazife, 'Rape in England between 1550–1770' in London Feminist History Group (ed.), *The Sexual Dynamics of History*, London, Pluto Press, 1983.

Bouce, Paul-Gabriel, *Sexuality in Eighteenth Century Britain*, Manchester, Manchester University Press, 1982.

Bristow, Edward J., *Vice and Vigilance: Purity Movements in Britain Since 1700*, Totowa, N.J., Rowman & Littlefield, 1977.

Brownmiller, Susan, *Against Our Will: Men, Women, and Rape*, London, Secker & Warburg, 1975.

Bularzik, Mary, 'Sexual Harassment at the Workplace: Historical Notes', *Radical America*, vol. 12, no. 4, July–August, 1978, 25–43.

Castle, Terry, 'Eros and Liberty at the English Masquerade, 1710–1790', *Eighteenth-Century Studies*, vol. 17, no. 2, Winter, 1983/1984, 162–81.

Chappell, Duncan, 'Cross Cultural Research in Forcible Rape', *International Journal of Crimonology and Penology*, vol. 4, 1976, 295–304.

Clark, Anna K., 'Rape or Seduction? A Controversy over Sexual Violence in the 19th Century', in London Feminist History Group (ed.), *The Sexual Dynamics of History*, London, Pluto Press, 1983.

Clark, Anna K., 'The Politics of Seduction in English Popular Culture, 1748–1848', in Jean Radford (ed.), *The Progress of Romance*, History Workshop Series, London, Routledge & Kegan Paul, 1986.

Clark, Lorenne M.G. and Lewis, Debra J., *Rape: the Price of Coercive Sexuality*, Toronto, the Women's Press, 1977.

Cott, Nancy, 'Passionlessness: an Interpretation of Victorian Sexual Ideology', *Signs* vol. 4, no. 2, 1978, 220–36.

Davidoff, Leonore, 'Class and Gender in Victorian England: the Diaries of Arthur J. Munby and Hannah Cullwick' in J.L. Newton, M.P. Ryan, and J.R. Walkowitz (eds), *Sex and Class in Women's History*, London, Routledge & Kegan Paul, 1983.

Davidoff, Leonore, 'Mastered for life: servant and wife in Victorian England', *Journal of Social History*, vol. 7, 1974, 406–28.

Davidoff, Leonore and Hall, Catherine, 'The Separation of Spheres, 1780–1850: Birmingham and East Anglia, Two Case Studies', Interim report, unpublished, University of Essex, 1980.

Dumaresq, Delia, 'Rape – Sexuality in the Law', *m/f*, Nos. 5 and 6, 1981, 41–59.

Edwards, Susan S.M., *Female Sexuality and the Law*, Oxford, Martin Robertson, 1981.

Ellis, Katherine, 'Charlotte Smith's Subversive Gothic', *Feminist Studies*, vol. 3, no. 3–4, Spring/Summer, 1976, 55–72.

Fairchilds, Cissie, 'Female Sexual Attitudes and the Rise of Illegitimacy: A Case Study', *Journal of Interdisciplinary History*, vol. 8, Spring, 1978, 627–67.

Finkelhor, David, *Sexually Victimized Children*, New York, Free Press, 1979.

Finnegan, Francis, *Poverty and Prostitution: A Study of Victorian Prostitutes in York*, Cambridge, Cambridge University Press, 1979.

Foucault, Michel, *The History of Sexuality*, vol. I, New York, Vintage, 1980.

Foucault, Michel (ed.), *I, Pierre Riviere . . .*, Harmondsworth, Penguin, 1975.

George, Dorothy, *London Life in the 18th Century*, Harmondsworth, Penguin, 1966 (1925).

Gillis, John, *Youth in History*, New York and London, Academic Press, 1974.

Gillis, John, 'Servants, Sexual Relations, and the Risks of Illegitimacy in London, 1801–1900' in J.L. Newton, M.P. Ryan, and J.R. Walkowitz (eds), *Sex and Class in Women's History*, London, Routledge & Kegan Paul, 1983.

Gillis, John, *For Better, for Worse: British Marriages, 1600 to the Present*, New York and Oxford, Oxford University Press, 1985.

Gordon, Linda, and O'Keefe, Paul, 'Incest as a form of family violence: evidence from historical case records', *Journal of Marriage and the Family*, February, 1984, pp. 27–34.

Gordon, Linda, and Dubois, Ellen, 'Seeking Ecstasy on the Battlefield: Danger and Pleasure in 19th century Feminist Thought' in Carole Vance (ed.), *Pleasure and Danger: Exploring Female Sexuality*, Boston, Routledge & Kegan Paul, 1984.

Gorham, Deborah, 'The Maiden Tribute of Modern Babylon Re-examined: child prostitution and the idea of childhood in late Victorian England', *Victorian Studies*, vol. 21, no. 3, Spring, 1978, 342–80.

Griffin, Susan, 'Rape, the All-American Crime', in Leroy Schultz (ed.), *Rape Victimology*, Springfield, Il., Chas C. Thomas, 1975.

Hall, Catherine, 'The Early Formation of Victorian Domestic Ideology' in Sandra Burman (ed.), *Fit Work for Women*, London, Croom Helm, 1979.

Hall, John (ed.), *Trial of Abraham Thornton*, Notable British Trial Series, London and Edinburgh, Wm. Hodge and Co, 1926.

Hamilton, Cecily, *Marriage as a Trade*, London, the Women's Press, 1981 (1909).

Hamilton, Marybeth, 'The life of a citizen in the hands of a woman: Sexual Assault in New York City, 1790–1820', Princeton University, 18 May 1984, unpublished paper.

Hanmer, Jalna, 'Violence and the Social Control of Women' in Feminist Anthology collective (ed.), *No Turning Back*, London, the Women's Press, 1981.

Hartmann, Heidi J. and Ross, Ellen, 'Comment on "On Writing the History of Rape" ', *Signs*, vol. III, no. 4, 1978, 931–5.

Hay, Douglas, 'Property, Authority and the Criminal Law' in D. Hay *et al.* (eds), *Albion's Fatal Tree*, London, Allen Lane, 1975.

Heineman, Helen, 'Frances Trollope's *Jessie Phillips*: Sexual Politics and the New Poor Law', *International Journal of Women's Studies*, vol. 1, 1978, 100–5.

Henriques, U.R.Q., 'Bastardy and the New Poor Law', *Past and Present*, no. 37, 1967, pp. 103–29.

Herman, Judith, with Hirschmann, Lisa, *Father-Daughter Incest*, Harvard University Press, 1981.

Hill, Christopher, 'Clarissa Harlowe and her times' in *Puritanism and Revolution*, London, Mercury Books, 1962 (1958).

Holloway, Wendy, '"I Just Wanted to Kill a Woman": Why? The Ripper and Male Sexuality', *Feminist Review*, vol. 9, Autumn, 1981, 33–40.

Jackson, Stevi, 'The Social Context of Rape: Sexual Scripts and Motivations', *Women's Studies International Quarterly*, vol. I, no. 1, 1978, 27–38.

Jacobus, Mary, 'Tess: the Making of a Pure Woman', in Susan Lipschitz (ed.), *Tearing the Veil: Essays in Femininity*, London, Routledge & Kegan Paul, 1978.

Jeffreys, Sheila, ' "Free from all uninvited touch of man": Women's Campaigns around Sexuality, 1800–1914', *Women's Studies International Forum*, 5 June 1982.

Lambertz, Janet R. 'Male-Female Violence in Late Victorian and Edwardian England', BA Honors Thesis, Cambridge, Mass., Harvard University, 1979.

Lambertz, Janet R., 'Sexual Harassment in the 19th-century English Cotton Industry', *History Workshop Journal*, 19, Spring, 1985, 29–61.

Lambertz, Janet R., 'The Politics and Economics of Family Violence in Liverpool, from the late 19th century to 1948', University of Manchester, M.Phil, 1984.

L'Esperance, Jean, 'Doctors and Women in Nineteenth Century Society: Sexuality and Role' in J. Woodward and D. Richards (eds), *Health Care and Popular Medicine in 19th Century England*,

London, Croom Helm, 1977.

Lester, D. 'Rape and Social Structures', *Psychological Reports*, vol. 35, 1974, 35.

Le Vine, R.A. 'Gusii Sex Offenses: a Study in Social Control', *American Anthropologist*, vol. 61, 1959, 965–90.

Lindemann, Barbara S., 'To Ravish and Carnally Know: Rape in 18th Century Massachusetts', *Signs*, vol. 10, no. 1, Autumn, 1984, 1–20.

London Rape Crisis Centre, *Sexual Violence: the Reality for Women*, London, the Women's Press, 1984.

McCalman, Iain, 'Unrespectable Radicalism: Infidels and Pornography in Early 19th Century London', *Past and Present*, No. 104, August 1984, 75–110.

Macintosh, Mary, 'Who Needs Prostitutes? The Ideology of Male Sexual Needs', in C. Smart and B. Smart (eds), *Women, Sexuality, and Social Control*, London, Routledge & Kegan Paul, 1978.

MacKinnon, Catherine A. *Sexual Harassment of Working Women: A Case of Sex Discrimination*, New Haven and London, Yale University Press, 1979.

MacKinnon, Catherine A., 'Feminism, Marxism, and the State: an Agenda for Theory', *Signs*, vol. 7, no. 3, 1982, 515–44.

MacKinnon, Catherine A., 'Feminism, Marxism, Method, and the State: Toward a Feminist Jurisprudence', *Signs* vol. 8, no. 4, 1983, 635–58.

Manchester, Colin, 'Obscenity Law Enforcement in the 19th Century', *Journal of Legal History*, vol. 2, May, 1981, 45–61.

Marcus, Steven, *The Other Victorians*, London, Weidenfeld & Nicolson, 1966.

Masson, Jeffrey Moussaieff, *The Assault on Truth: Freud's Suppression of the Seduction Theory*, Harmondworth, Penguin, 1985.

Medea, A. and Thompson, K., *Against Rape*, New York, Farrar, Strauss, and Giroux, 1974.

Mitchell, Sally, 'The forgotten female of the period: penny weekly family magazines of the 1830s and 1840s' in Martha Vicinus (ed.), *A Widening Sphere*, Bloomington, Ind., Indiana University Press, 1978.

Mrazek, Patricia Beezley, 'Definition and Recognition of Sexual Child Abuse: Historical and Cultural Perspectives' in P.B. Mrazek and C. Henry Kempe (eds), *The Sexual Abuse of Children*, Oxford, Pergamon, 1981.

Olson, Ruth A. 'Rape: an "Unvictorian" Aspect of Life in Upper Canada', *Ontario History*, vol. 68, no. 2, June, 1976, 75–9.

Pattullo, Polly, *Judging Women*, London, National Council for Civil Liberties, 1983.

Pinchbeck, Ivy, *Women Workers and the Industrial Revolution, 1750–1850*, London, Virago, 1981 (1930).

Pinchbeck, Ivy, and Hewitt, Margaret, *Children in English Society*, Vols. I and II, London, Routledge & Kegan Paul, 1969, 1973.

Plaza, Monique, 'Our Costs and Their Benefits', *m/f*, vol. 4, 1980, 28–39.

Pleck, Elizabeth, 'Feminist responses to crimes against women, 1868–1896', *Signs*, vol. 8, no. 3, Spring, 1983, 450–70.

Post, J.B., 'Ravishment of Women and the Statute of Westminster' in J.H. Baker (ed.), *Legal Records and the Historian*, London, Royal Historical Society, 1978.

Quaife, G.R., *Wanton Wenches and Wayward Wives*, London, Croom Helm, 1979.

Ross, Ellen, 'Fierce Questions and Taunts: Married Life in London between the Wars', *Feminist Studies*, vol. 8, no. 3, Fall, 1982, 572–602.

Ross, Ellen, and Rapp, Rayna, 'Sex and Society: a Research Note from Social History and Anthropology', *Comparative Studies in Society and History*, vol. 23, no. 1, January, 1981, 51–72.

Rossiaud, Jacques, 'Prostitution, Youth, and Society in the Towns of Southeastern France in the Fifteenth Century' in R. Forster and O. Ranum (eds), *Deviants and the Abandoned in French Society*, Baltimore, Johns Hopkins University Press, 1978.

Ruggiero, Guido, 'Sexual Criminality in the Early Renaissance, 1338–1358', *Journal of Social History*, vol. 8, Summer, 1975, 18–37.

Ruggiero, Guido, *Violence in Early Renaissance Venice*, New Brunswick, Rutgers University Press, 1980.

Rush, Florence, *The Best Kept Secret: The Sexual Abuse of Children*, New York, Prentice-Hall, 1980.

Ryan, Mary P., 'The Power of Women's Networks: a Case Study of Female Moral Reform in Antebellum America', *Feminist Studies*, vol. V, no. 1, Spring, 1979, 66–85.

Schwendinger, Julia R. and Herman, *Rape and Inequality*, Beverly Hills, Sage, 1983.

Shorter, Edward, 'On Writing the History of Rape', *Signs*, vol. 3, 1977, 471–82.

Smart, Carol, and Smart, Barry, *Women, Sexuality and Social Control*, London, Routledge & Kegan Paul, 1978.

Smith, F. Barry, 'Sexuality in Britain, 1800–1900: Some Suggested Revisions' in Martha Vicinus (ed.), *A Widening Sphere*, Bloomington, Indiana, Indiana University Press, 1977.

Stanley, Liz, (ed.), *The Diaries of Hannah Cullwick, Victorian Maidservant*, London, Virago, 1984.

Stansell, Christine, *Women of the Poor in Federalist and Early National New York*, forthcoming.

Staves, Susan, 'British Seduced Maidens', *Eighteenth Century Studies*, vol. 14, no. 2, Winter, 1980–1, 109–34.

Storch, Robert, 'Police Control of Street Prostitution in Victorian London' in D.H. Bayley, (ed.), *Police and Society*, Beverly Hills/London, Sage Publications, 1977.

Svalastaga, K., 'Rape and Social Structure', *Pacific Sociological Review*, vol. 5, 1962, 48–53.

Taylor, Barbara, *Eve and the New Jerusalem: Socialism and Feminism in The 19th Century*, New York, Pantheon, 1983.

Thorsler, Peter L., 'Incest as a Romantic Symbol', *Comparative Literature Studies*, vol. 2, 1965, 41–58.

Tomes, Nancy, 'A Torrent of Abuse: Crimes of Violence between Working-Class Men and Women in Lonodn, 1840–1875', *Journal of Social History*, vol.11, 1978, 328–45.

Toner, Barbara, *The Facts of Rape*, London, Hutchinson, 1977.

Trudgill, Eric, 'Prostitution and Paterfamilias' in H.J. Dyos and M. Wolff (eds), *The Victorian City*, vol. II, London, Routledge & Kegan Paul, 1973.

Voloshinov, V.N., *Marxism and the Philosophy of Language*, New York, Seminar Press, 1973.

Walkowitz, Judith R., *Prostitution and Victorian Society: Women, Class, and State*, Cambridge, Cambridge University Press, 1980.

Walkowitz, Judith R., 'Jack the Ripper and the Myth of Male Violence', *Feminist Studies*, vol. 8, no. 3, Fall, 1982, 543–74.

Webster, Paula, 'The Politics of Rape in Primitive Societies', *Heresies*, No. 6, Summer, 1978, 16–22.

Weber, Donna Lee, 'Fair Game: Rape and sexual aggression in some early 18th century prose', University of Toronto Ph.D, 1980.

Weeks, Jeffrey, *Sex, Politics and Society: The Regulation of Sexuality Since 1800*, London, Longman, 1981.

Young, Kate, and Harris, Olivia, 'The Subordination of Women in Cross-Cultural Perspecive' in *Papers on Patriarchy*, Brighton, Women's Publishing Collective, 1976.

Index

Other Pandora titles

THE SPINSTER AND HER ENEMIES

Feminism and Sexuality 1890 to 1930

Sheila Jeffreys

It is generally accepted by traditional historical interpreters, that the sexual puritanism of Victorian England gave way to the first 'sexual revolution' of the twentieth century. Sheila Jeffreys presents a different thesis which she supports with a wealth of evidence.

She examines the activities of feminist campaigners around such issues as child abuse and prostitution and assesses how these campaigns shaped social purity in the 1880s and 1890s. She demonstrates how the work of sexologists such as Carpenter and Havelock Ellis undermined and attacked the thriving, militant feminism of the late nineteenth and early twentieth centuries and asserts that the decline of this feminism was due largely to the promotion of a sexual ideology which was hostile to women's independence.

0 86358 050 5   History
252pp paperback

WORKING YOUR WAY TO THE BOTTOM

The Feminization of Poverty

Hilda Scott

The 'new poor' of today are invisible.
They are also women.

It is a special kind of poverty, the causes of which are not fully understood by most men working in official and unofficial poverty research. Hilda Scott argues that they are blinded by assumptions about 'women's place' to the work that women actually do and the incomes they actually receive. For example, is a secretary considered working class if married to an assembly line worker but middle class if married to an accountant? And what happens if she is divorced from the accountant?

Hilda Scott produces startling evidence to prove that women the world over are rapidly becoming the 'new poor'. She argues that unless there is a radical re-think of economic policy women will keep on 'working their way to the bottom'.

0 86358 011 4   General/Contemporary political and economic issues
192pp paperback

MOST DANGEROUS WOMEN

Feminist Peace Campaigners of the Great War

Anne Wiltsher

The women of Greenham are the latest in a long line of women who have dedicated themselves to the cause of peace. Half the leading women of the British suffrage movement opposed the First World War. Working through the international women's suffrage movement, they linked up with other feminists in Europe and America and tried to push the men in power towards a negotiated peace.

Anne Wiltsher follows the extraordinary exploits of these women in *Most Dangerous Women*. She brings to life the central characters in the drama, describing their determination to cross international borders despite war-time travel restrictions, their encounters with leading statesmen, their vilification by the press and the public, their philosophies and friendships.

0 86358 010 6   History
288pp paperback

DISCOVERING WOMEN'S HISTORY

A Practical Manual

Deirdre Beddoe

Rainy Sunday afternoons, long winter evenings: why not set yourself
a research project, either on your own or in a group or classroom?
This is the message from Deirdre Beddoe, an historian who tears
away the mystique of her own profession in this step-by-step guide
to researching the lives of ordinary women in Britain from 1800 to
1945. *Discovering Women's History* tells you how to get started on the
detective trail of history and how to stalk your quarry through attics
and art galleries, museums and old newspapers, church archives and
the Public Records Office – and how to publish your findings once
you have completed your project.

'an invaluable and fascinating guide to the raw material for anyone
approaching this unexplored territory.'   *The Sunday Times*

'Thrilling and rewarding and jolly good fun.'   *South Wales Argus*

0-86358-008-4   Hobbies/Social History
232pp 198 × 129 mm illustrated

THE DORA RUSSELL READER

57 Years of Writing and Journalism 1925-1982

Dora Russell

Dora Russell is one of the most remarkable women of this century.
Her extraordinary life and work can now be appreciated in this, the
first collection of her writings and journalism.

Dora Russell has campaigned tirelessly for peace since the First
World War. In the 1950s she took the women's Caravan of Peace
into Eastern Europe. In the 1980s she is as active as ever, as her
passionate 1982 article on *The Challenge of Humanism in the Nuclear
Age* demonstrates.

This book introduces a new generation to the powerful mix of
intellect and compassion in the work of this courageous woman.

0–86358-020-3   Politics/Feminism
242pp paperback

MY COUNTRY IS THE WHOLE WORLD

An Anthology of Women's Work on Peace and War

Cambridge Women's Peace Collective (eds)

Women's struggle for peace is no recent phenomenon. In this book, the work of women for peace from 600 BC to the present is documented in a unique collection of extracts from songs, poems, diaries, letters, petitions, pictures, photographs and pamphlets through the ages. A book to give as a gift, to read aloud from, to research from, to teach from, *My Country is the Whole World* is both a resource and an inspiration for all who work for peace today.

'an historic document . . . readers will be amazed at the extent of the collection.'   *Labour Herald*

'a beautifully presented and illustrated book which makes for accessible and enlightening reading.'   *Morning Star*

0-86358-004-1   Social Questions/History
306pp A5 illustrated throughout paperback

TIME AND TIDE WAIT FOR NO MAN

The Story of a Feminist Political Weekly in the 1920s

Dale Spender

The magazine *Time and Tide* was founded as a feminist political weekly in 1920 by women who had been active in the battle for women's suffrage. It was to be a magazine run by women, for women, which would keep a sharp eye out for national and international developments as they affected women.

Its founders and contributors included Rebecca West and her sister Laetita Fairfield, Cicely Hamilton, Emma Goldman, Vera Brittain, Winifred Holtby and Crystal Eastman.

Dale Spender takes us on a narrated journey through selections from the first fifteen years of *Time and Tide*.

0-86358-024-6   Social History/Women's Studies
287pp paperback